SCAPEGOAT

AND

OTHER

POEMS

SCAPEGOAT AND OTHER POEMS

WAKE FOREST UNIVERSITY PRESS

ALAN GILLIS

ISBN 978-1-930630-80-2 (paperback)

Library of Congress Control Number 2016941912

Designed and typeset by Quemadura

Publication of this book was generously

supported by the Boyle Family Fund.

ACKNOWLEDGMENTS: This volume is a compendium of poems written from 2000 to 2014.
All poems have previously been published by The Gallery Press in Ireland. The poems from
"The Ulster Way" to "Progress" are taken from *Somebody, Somewhere* (2004); from "Lagan
Weir" to "Laganside" from *Hawks and Doves* (2007); from "Eloquence" to "*from* Here Comes
the Night" from *Here Comes the Night* (2010); and from "August in Edinburgh" to "The Sweep-
ing" from *Scapegoat* (2014). Many thanks to Peter Fallon.

CONTENTS

SCAPEGOAT AND OTHER POEMS

THE ULSTER WAY

This is not about burns or hedges.
There will be no gorse. You will not
notice the ceaseless photosynthesis
or the dead tree's thousand fingers,
the trunk's inhumanity writhing with texture,
as you will not be passing into farmland.
Nor will you be set upon by cattle,

ingleberried, haunching and haunting
with their eyes, their shocking opals,
graving you, hoovering and scooping you,
full of a whatness that sieves you through
the abattoir hillscape, the runnel's slabber
through darkgrass, sweating for the night
that will purple to a love-bitten bruise.

All this is in your head. If you walk,
don't walk away, in silence, under the stars'
ice-fires of violence, to the water's darkened strand.
For this is not about horizons, or their curving
limitations. This is not about the rhythm
of a songline. There are other paths to follow.
Everything is about you. Now listen.

12TH OCTOBER, 1994

I enter the Twilight Zone,
    the one run
by Frankie 'Ten Pints' Fraser, and slide the heptagon
    of my twenty
pence piece into its slot. The lights come on.
    Sam the Sham
and the Pharaohs are playing *Wooly Bully*.

A virtual combat zone lights up the green
    of my eyes,
my hand clammy on the joystick, as Johnny 'Book
    Keeper' McFeeter
saunters in and Smokey sings *The Tracks of My Tears*.
    He gives the nod
to Betty behind the bulletproof screen.

Love of my life he says, and she says
    ach Johnny,
when who do you know but Terry 'The Blaster' McMaster
    levels in
and B Bumble and The Stingers start playing *Nut Rocker*.
    I shoot down
a sniper and enter a higher level.

Betty buzzes Frankie who has a shifty
    look around,
poking his nut around a big blue door, through which
    I spy
Billy 'Warts' McBreeze drinking tea and tapping his toes
    to Randy
and The Rainbows' version of *Denise*.

On the screen I mutilate a double-agent
    Ninja and collect
a bonus drum of kerosene. *The Game of Love* by Wayne
    Fontana pumps
out of the machine, when I have to catch my breath,
    realizing Ricky
'Rottweiler' Rice is on my left

saying watch for the nifty fucker
    with the cross-
bow on the right. Sweat-purls tease my spine, tensed ever
    more rigidly,
when Ricky's joined by Andy 'No Knees' Tweed,
    both of them
whistling merrily to The Crystals' *Then He Kissed Me.*

What the fuck is going on
    here asks
Victor 'Steel Plate' Hogg, as he slides through the fire
    door. The kid's

on level 3, says Andy. At which point Frankie does his nut,
    especially since
The Cramps are playing *Can Your Pussy Do the Dog?*

Betty puts on Curtis and the Clichés'
    Brush Against Me
Barbarella instead, when the first helicopter shreds the air
    to the left
of the screen. Gathering my wits and artillery, I might eclipse
    the high score
of Markie 'Life Sentence' Prentice, set on October 6th.

I hear Benny 'Vindaloo' McVeigh say
    right we're going
to do this fucking thing. By now the smoke is so thick
    the screen is almost grey.
The Shangri-Las are playing *Remember (Walkin' in the Sand)*.
    Frankie says
no, Victor, nobody's going to fucking disband.

Bob B Soxx and The Blue Jeans are playing
    Zip-A-Dee-Doo-Dah.
Through a napalm blur I set the interns free. They wear US
    marine khaki.
Jimmy 'Twelve Inch' Lynch says son, not bad for 20p.
    I leave the Zone and go
back to the fierce grey day. It looks like snow.

TO BELFAST

May your bulletproof knickers drop like rain
and your church-spires attain a higher state of grace.
My lily-of-the-valley, the time is at hand
to ring your bells and uproot your cellulose stem.
I bought hardware, software, and binoculars to trace
your ways of taking the eyes from my head.

And none of it worked. We've been coming to a head
for too long; aircraft prick the veins of your rain-
bow as they shoot you in soft focus to trace
the tramlines of your cellulite skin. But with the grace
of a diva on a crackling screen, you never stem
to their cameras, you're forever getting out of hand.

Once in school, on a greaseproof page, we had to trace
the busts and booms of your body, and I was ashamed to hand
mine in because it lacked what Da called grace.
And I wish I was the centre of a rain-
drop that's falling on your head, the key to your hand-
cuffs, the drug that could re-conjugate your head.

For Belfast, if you'd be a Hollywood film, then I'd be Grace
Kelly on my way to Monaco, to pluck the stem

of a maybell with its rows of empty shells, its head
of one hundred blinded eyes. I would finger your trace
in that other city's face, and bite its free hand
as it fed me, or tried to soothe the stinging of your rain.

DON'T YOU

1

I was working as a waitress in a cocktail bar,
that much is true. But even then I knew I'd find
myself behind the wheel of a large automobile,
or in a beautiful house, asking myself, well,
if sweet dreams are made of these, why don't I travel
the world and the seven seas to Rio, and dance there
in the sand, just like a river twisting through the dusty land?
For though you thought you were my number one,
this girl did not want to have a gun for hire,
no bright-spark who was just dancing in the dark.

2

You were working as a waitress in a cocktail bar,
when I met you, and I believed in miracles:
every step you took, I was watching you.
I asked for your name, tipped you again and again
and you said, Don't—don't you want me
to fetch you a drink that would turn your pink mouth blue?
Don't you think this tenth tiny chaser is ten times bigger than you?
Don't you talk about places and people you will never know.
Don't you symbolize femininity by use of the letter O.
And I said, Don't you want me, baby? Don't you want me . . .

DELIVERANCE

Even the trees are on something.
Somebody, somewhere, is almost
making love. Clouds target the hillside.
Leaves are trapped by the bars
of their branches and airplanes
guard the blue, as you try to break through
the green prison of your eyes.
Everyone is going to get off.

⌐

Unfortunately there are no positions left
he said. For the record, what can you do?
Somebody, somewhere, is making a killing.
Cigars leer across barstools, asking for a light
now the Sky™ has been taken from your house.
Then a briefcase tries to sell you up the river.
You shoot the breeze. He talks of a message:
there'd be something in it, all you need do is deliver.

⌐

The addicted trees are hooked
on the air. Somebody, somewhere,

is inventing a cure.
Everyone inside is bustling to break out
and the sun has served its time.
Wet dreamers of wide profit margins
drive below the golfball moon,
their speakers selling them life
style options, while you are lying
low. Thieves and lovers gamble in your eyes.

There is a rustling without the windows,
a tinkling in your ear. And somebody,
somewhere, is saved by a machine.
In your dreams you speak to free
heartbeats, dipsticks, ice flows, smart bombs,
moon men, wolfhounds, death pints,
blue chips, close weather, stem cells, burning discs
and world wide searches. You speak of bonds.

You wake behind the sun and make
your delivery. There is nothing
in it. The ground beneath your feet
rotates. The planes are on patrol.
Something flies into the pane and dies.

A breeze blows in and everyone profits.
Somebody, somewhere, will understand.
Rub the blue eyes of your windows.
Love is making trees.
You are green under turquoise skies.

When you walked with her you walked into vespers
and dusklight below the lapwing's ululation,
indigo skies, lost to the signatures
of the river, its phantom syncopation
pouring cantatas into the chalice
of her ear—through the mascara-ringed moons
of her eyes, malice
through the looking glass, that music loomed.

When she made a beeline for your bed
your numberless nights were almost numbered
as you tried to enter the crunch of her head,
the sardonyx of her eyes, the amber
of her pelt, her thighs' riverbed—
swinging your huckleboned rumba
on the buttermilk cotton of her bed—
until the morning found you, wildly encumbered.

There were times when you felt you could rip through
the night, that the hug-me-tight
leather of the night
would unzip and pour you
an Absolut vodka and lime
as you drank in the calamine
and hairspray, darkshade and tubelight,
your eyes big-widened screens of skybright blue.

She said goodnight sweetheart, it's time to go
where the sky is always blue and you can't hear
the river because the river always flows
in time with the constant atmosphere
that half-forms and tingles mind and throat
in measure with the treeshade and tambourine leaves,
the crow-picker's lustration of the whiskey-tinctured eaves,
and not the flimflam and jissom of these indifferent notes.

In your dreams her eyes mellowed into milk
and Kahlua,
she plunged the queensize sea of her silk
bed like a dolphin, dancing hula-hulas
until you awakened to a sky of ocean blue,
drinking volcanic water with Tesco's Finest Earl Grey
as yellowhammers loitered in darkgreen bridleways
on a screensaver that stayed the night for you.

On other nights you writhed in the dankness of your bed,
a writhing seedbed of termites
that chawed on your eyeballs, your fetid cheese head,
welting you in the molar crunch of the night,
melting you to corpse juice and meat rot,
death bones and finity and forget-me-nots
igniting you from toetip to head,
a red-whipped bushfire of wild-lipped lovebites.

You would find yourself driving through
dark winding roads, sycamore groves
under an inconstant sky: chameleon grey and greengrey,
carrot, heather, mushroom and ivory,
almond green, lavender, peach-bloom and jasmine,
khaki-flecked, claret, oyster pink and citron,
constantly changing from dove to duck-egg-speckled,
quilted in caramel, biscuit, petrol blue and gun metal.

You parked to walk by the river, initially in time
with the bubble and rush of its fishscale lather,
but soon you were lost in the bluegrass pantomine
of slurp and bebble and girny-gab glissando,
stopped short by its doo-wop, its pizz-popping jingle-jangle
as its velocious surface of calypso ripple-current
puggled up a torrent in a billow-warped refrain,
yammering to rigadoons of light vibronic rain.

You turned away to climb the hillcap
where the river couldn't reach—through feverfew
and agrimony, the submarine shit slaps
of snuffle-steaming heifers, where the ash and ember
coloured town, its diminishing corrugations,
fumed below the landfall and vapour trails—
wondering, as the spoilt sun yoked the sky,
what you'd see if you could see through her eyes.

You saw a deathtoll carved in the middle road,
the numbers zip-filed, downloaded holes in the night
where peace bombs slept behind the schoolyard fence
and cadavers flared their teeth in self-defence;
watched over by satellite,
you took a heavy-booted saunter through demeaning fields
to where morning broke, the sky became lychee,
the sun's head served on the platter of the sea.

Some day you would wake and find yourself dead
by the river, the multitasking trees,
zephyrs rubbing salt into your hardboiled head
beneath a big blue sky, collapsing to the sea,
the river, river, easing through your bones,
turning to the town at last with ghost-drafts
of wisdom, breathing 'blessed shall they be
who give your children grass instead of stones'.

And so you tumbled down the hillside lurching
hither and thither until you finally ran aground,
where you awakened to feel your head without touching
on the outskirts of town, and you found,
beneath the big blue sky, a river flowing into sound
among whin burns and hazels, never to know
what might be benamed and behappened below
the still breathing sky, where the river runs its round.

PROGRESS

They say that for years Belfast was backwards
and it's great now to see some progress.
So I guess we can look forward to taking boxes
from the earth. I guess that ambulances
will leave the dying back amidst the rubble
to be explosively healed. Given time,
one hundred thousand particles of glass
will create impossible patterns in the air
before coalescing into the clarity
of a window. Through which, a reassembled head
will look out and admire the shy young man
taking his bomb from the building and driving home.

LAGAN WEIR

The way things are going,
    there'll be no quick fix, no turning
back the way that flock of starlings
    skirls back on itself then swerves forward,
swabbing and scrawling the shell-pink
    buffed sky, while I stand in two minds
on this scuffed bridge leaning over
    the fudged river that slooshes its dark way
to open harbours and the glistering sea.

Like flak from fire, a blizzard of evacuees,
    that hula-hooping sky-swarm of starlings
swoops and loops the dog rose sky,
    while any way I look the writing's
on the wall. I watch the hurly-burlyed,
    humdrummed traffic belch to a stop,
fugging, clacking, charring the clotted air,
    making it clear things are going to get
a whole lot worse before they get better.

That flickered, fluttered hurry scurry
    of starlings sweeps left, then swishes right
through the violet sky while I huddle
    and huff, with a dove in one ear saying

look the other way, a hawk in the other
    braying self-righteous fury. It's hard
not to turn back to a time when one look
    at you and I knew things were going to get
a whole lot better before they'd get worse.

That hue and cry, those hurricanes
    of starlings swoosh and swirl their fractals
over towers, hotels, hospitals, flyovers,
    catamarans, city-dwellers, passers-through,
who might as well take a leap and try following
    after that scatter wheeling circus of shadows
as slowly turn and make their dark way
    homeward, never slowing, not knowing
the way things are going.

FROM ON A WEEKEND BREAK IN A POLITICAL VACUUM

To bugger off completely and drive north,
the breaking ocean on one side a tide
of greenblack rucks and rollings,
stormblown buoys and blue water lights
waved beneath a V of whooper swans
gliding into the hoar-lit horizon.

After reaching her rented cottage
she inhales the dusked air, then blows
it out, wrapped in woollywarm jim-jams
with iced whiskey, magazines and the crash-
splashed, long, withdrawing roar of the sea
rasping behind loose-rattled windows.

To get away, escape the boo-hoos,
tweets and managers, usernames,
traffic and troubles, the death toll
of twenty-four hour news, she fogs
her mind on a mountain of catalogues,
travel brochures, *Chill-out Classics II*.

Brad Pitt and Angelina Jolie are helping
children in Africa. The photo is so
beautiful, they float free from themselves,

free from the photo's frame, blue eyes,
brilliant hair adrift over hills, over the sea.
She follows but falls, into the sea.

If she could only catch hold of herself
or seize each pulsed wave and mazed
aftermath twisting through her mind
she might know what to do, who to be,
the way things are. But everything glitters
for an instant and then snuffs it.

An expert in *Time* says the earth is all ground
zero now, and she knows there's nowhere to go
but still, she'll follow the glint of sorrel-
coated horses bounding through unhedged
greens towards blue surveilled horizons
hearing river water running underground.

She knows there's nothing to do but try
and learn to love the spray of the coast's
frowsty smacks of fast mazarine air,
privet and firethorn, the wind-rushed
barley and angelica, poplar groves
under the peach-blushed and gull-charged sky.

Like a child crying over a clump
of broken dolls, hoping to unmurder,
she'll watch the endless waves reach

their limits, and walk through phantom air,
its contagion of blue, as starlings flusker
and flitch over fields of low barley

through gobsmacked garnet skies,
to alight on numbered trees, bursting out
of themselves, straining to reach up to
the death-flare of the sun, which multiplies.
But, for now, she lies back to sleep and dream,
enjoy the weekend. There is work to do.

IN HER ROOM ON A
LIGHT-KISSED AFTERNOON

Not only the nip and tuck of her skin quilting
milk bent bones; not only the somersaulting
head spin of her light skin spread atilt
the deep of her lemon-puffed pillow and quilt
lifting into the citron-charged air; but even the lilt
of strings from the speaker on her well-built
mockernut cabinet, the light from her half-
opened window and the high heckled laugh
of girls promenading past her bedroom,
scrickety-screeching over each other's lampoon
of a pizza-faced boy they tortured all afternoon;
even the snow-capped peaks of her importune
shoulder-bones, the squidged soles of her feet,
the daylight's tufts in the meadowsweet
sky charged with godwits, lemon-puffed billows
and Boeings: all these things sink below
her arse-through-mouth fear of the aeroplane's *kaboom*,
its flaring nose dive-bombing her bedroom;
her fear of turning cloud, her skin become cotton,
a lemon-puffed pastry shred to pieces in the rotten
sky and windblown, turned to tears
cut like arrowheads, salt-fired and clear,
pitter-patter-clattering her window

as I plunge her lip-stained pillow
and quilt, her light citrus skin
with hate mail, emissions, election results breaking in
as we lie there, beating, dead to our bones
in her lemon-puffed bower of words, and sticks, and stones.

AMONG THE BARLEY

We met at the tail of a check-out queue
and when she turned her head she spread
like blood through snowflakes, all melt and fire,
as my ripe tomatoes tumbled to the floor.
And when she bared her chamomile thighs,
her red-toed sunblaze, my body became
barley fields on fire. My frazzled ears roared.
My old house flared to fizz-burned bananas,
red meat frizzle-zings, the attic razed to hell,
and I knelt at the doorway singing High Hosannas.

⌐

After she'd cut her doorkey and laid out
blueprints of her kitchen cupboards' insides
I felt deep-bosomed, big-bellied and wide
as a turnip field, days before harvest.
I bought walking boots and walked through river-
wound groves. I bought allegories of birth
and death, framed them, and drilled them to
her wall. And how they fell. When she entered
a room eyes swivelled and bulged for her,
red crab-apples craving for the earth.

◣

For you, I wanted to leaf and take root.
So I stood firm and pulled my lips full gape,
wanting to mouth apples. *Uaugghh.* I *uaugghh*ed
nothing until it hurt. And then I surrendered.
Orchards of apples began to appear—
pear-shaped, plum-coloured, pineapple-dappled.
My eyes turned seed, my veins fructosed
and my mouth bloomed stem-twigs for sound
and wounded fruit for sense, gulping forth
a juiced-up speech, or merely talking apples.

◣

I slap a second lick of banana dream gloss
on the back room's walls while you measure
the cove for hanging your unframed mirror.
Soon we'll discuss our diaries, looking for
windows when we can next DIY together.
The forecast is for spells of lower pressure.
I finger-slick sweat from your pent shoulders
as the sun leaks onto the living room floor
to trickle down thighs and thrawn limbs—
barley sheaves waiting for the thresher.

◣

We walk a line that curves from day
to day, often squiggly, higgledy-piggledy
as if etch-a-sketched by a sugar-rushed
two-year-old, so that I find myself
rushing through a maze of malls, esplanades,
restaurants, barley fields, beds, lakeside
pathways, garden patios with sundials—
meeting points that blend and deepen
and brighten and bloom the way a room
looks bigger when you've been in it for a while.

⌐

We meant to make love on the stairs,
the deskchair, the windowsill, the throw
your sister brought back from Brazil.
Now we zigzag and busy-buzz by
one another like honey bees snuffing
pollen in the autumnal red and gold glare.
So let our love be watertight and let
the breeze blow through it. Let us be solid
oak and fluid. Let us be truth, let us be dare,
the swallow's dive sculpted into rock, and air.

CARNIVAL

Black buffed leather-tongued brogues with oat-
meal socks and khaki y-fronts, pleated slacks,
pert navy and gold striped double-windsored tie
on a twill non-iron white hassle-free shirt,
stiff blazer, wool felt bowler, dead white
gloves and orange sash with silver tassels,
marching onward, left, right, elbows tight
to lambegs, banners, fifes, rows of waving
wives, marching onward, in formation, marching
on a Judas nation by the Queen's highway,
the town's High Street, roundabouts where forked
roads meet and never yield, marching to the field
of battle, field of peace, field patrolled by plain-
clothed police; field of Jesus, field of hope, field
of Bush and fuck the Pope; marching onward into
heaven to scourge its halls of unwashed brethren;
then a blue bus home, content with your labours,
to watch *Countdown* and your favourite, *Neighbours.*

BOB THE BUILDER IS A DICKHEAD

Some night when you're lost in a nest of narrow lanes
and forgotten where you've come from, where you're going, again,

you'll think back and thank me for when you were three
and I threw out all of your Bob the Builder DVDs.

I'm telling you now—Scoop, Dizzy, Lofty,
Muck and Rolly will make you soft and we

can't have you thinking you can fix it
every time the fan is hit with flying horse shit.

They want you to believe you should work for the team,
sacrifice yourself to a starched-collar dream,

but here's your choice: be shat upon or look out for No. 1;
either kick against the pricks, or else become one.

Balamory's full of Torys! Silence the Fat Controller
imposing his order on the island of Sodor!

But don't go bawling, this isn't doomsday,
it's simply better things are spelled out this way.

For example, sex.
Pick up what you can at the local multiplex,

for soon your sanity will rely on
how well you placate your wee pyjama python.

Soon you'll do anything for your love's furry mouse,
so take her to Paris, or your favourite curry house

and buy her a lamb balti with a Cobra or Tiger,
rub her happy thigh as you sit down beside her,

but fastforward the scene by a couple of years
and you'll have nothing but Yesterday between your ears.

She'll have left you hopped-up, gormless, parched,
just one more wrinkle on the arse.

You'll want to whisk back on a magical broom
to that mystic split-second of your fusion in the womb:

to fly through celestial chaos, that cosmic hootenanny,
and find the divine factory where they sort out pricks from fannies.

There, you'll seek the management office in order to destroy
the Goddess of Creation—who'll be announcing over the tannoy

with flat-packed officiousness:
'Welcome customers! On entering consciousness,

please proceed directly to an impasse and fill
out a complaint form.' For this is Mission Impossible:

think positive, think negative—whatever you reckon,
your thoughts will self-destruct in fifteen seconds.

You'll end up on your knees seeking Holy Communion,
a taxpaying citizen of a multinational union.

Your American landlord will swing by in his Lexus,
take all your money then fuck off back to Texas.

You might move from place to place, a mind-boggled rover,
or stay in Belfast where, although the war is over

the Party of Bollocks and the party of Balls
are locked in battle for the City Hall.

Even if you roam, you'll find it difficult
to avoid starvation and its twin, the cult

of profit backed by death planes firing vanity,
base rates, trigger-fingered inanity.

But, of course, I might be wrong. Perhaps a constant
path exists for the fearless itinerant

to tread where, on the threshold of heaven,
the figures in the street become the figures of heaven

and our ears will alloy the preposterous babble.
One thing's for sure, every step will be a gamble.

Will it be paper, scissors, or stone?
Take another throw, son, of the devil's bones.

THE LAD

I spend my days drinking beneath
the bar's plasma screen, checking out
the Czech waitress, all tits and teeth.
And when I hear someone splitting hairs,
antsy with a world of cares about the rights
and wrongs of the war, or whether
the fulltime score fairly reflected the game,
I wade in and tell them 'pity the man
unsure of his name', then leave them
to brood, secure in my manhood.

I pay my way, walk out to the carpark,
and with my right hand I grip my Adam's whip,
my hazel wand, my straw-haired vagabond,
my Pirate of Penzance, my lilac love lance,
my ramrod, my wad, my schlong, my tube, my tonk,
my Jimmy, my Johnny, my tarse, my verge, my honk,
my bishop, my pawn, my rook, my king, my knight,
my chairman of the board, my stranger in the night,
my Gonzo, my Kermie, my Bert, my Ernie,
my weenie, my weener, my Mr Misdemeanour,

my chopper, my boffer, my chantilly lace-loving big bopper,
my porridge pipe, my yellow and ripe

banana, my iguana, my nerve-ends of Nirvana,
my snuffer, my chuffer, my duffer, my stuffer,
my Black and Decker, my donut inspector,
my dickery-dock, my Geronimo's tomahawk,
my tinkle, my sprinkle, my Rip Van Winkle,
my Mad Max, my Crazy Mick, my dip-, my wiggle-, my pogo-stick,
my hawk, my dove, my love-
bomb bazooka, my squinty-eyed scheming pooka,

my Chief Whip, my guv, my middle man in the transactions of love,
my hootchie-cootchie tickler, my sporty little ripper,
my virginia creeper, my heat seeker,
my Best, my Law, my Charlton, my Stiles,
my volatile erstwhile fertile mobile projectile,
my d'Artagnan, my explorer of the canyon,
my saxophone, my knick-knack-paddy-whack, my dog and my bone,
my saucisson, my saveloy, my knackwurst, my donger,
my Pinocchio's nose growing longer, and longer,
my high and flighty piccolo, my 'just popped out to say hello',

my Hans Solo, my Marco Polo, is this the way to Amarillo?,
my zoot-suited rooter, my hooter, my trusty pee-shooter,
my custard marrow, my Zeno's arrow, my submarine descending the
    abyssal plain's narrows,
my Emperor Ming, my Lord of the Rings,
my pintle, my pizzle, my bringer of the drizzle,
my Spade, my Holmes, my Marlowe, my Wimsey,

my dawn-raid, my dome, my sparrow, my flip-flop-flimsy,
my sweet disorder in the dress, my six-million dollar man (more or less),
my Viceroy, my land ahoy, my wild colonial boy,
my noble Lord issuing like Radiant Hesper when his golden hayre in
    th'Ocean billowes he hath Bathed fayre,

my busker in the subway, my folksinger, my ring-a-ling-a-ding-dong-dinger,
my tomatoes and cucumber, my lucky bingo number,
my blubber, my flubber, my slippy-dippy rubberdubber,
my pepperoni rollarama, my wildebeest grazing on the plains of the
    savannah,
my great rooted blossomer, my limp father of thousands,
my bearded iris that brought forth buds, and bloomed blossoms, and
    yielded almonds,
my curious Hobbit, my John Wayne Bobbit;
and with my goose-pimpled bum against my Nissan's bonnet,
my one-eyed zipper fish blows an angel's kiss
as I hit-and-miss into the tax disc of the sun.

DRIVING HOME

I saw it coming, as I zipped and vroomed
headward from Coleraine to Belfast
under phone masts and sycamores
arching the flat road's tunnel through
hayfields, sun-gilt and harvests, my red
car careening in a fifth gear of freedom
past other cars' carbon fart trails,
cloudsmoked brushstrokes over scumbled
green horizons, every driver shooting
the bluetooth breeze with front windows
rolled to share their iPods' perfect playlists.

I saw it coming, as I left behind
the office and to-do lists; my boss, my other
boss, the other one again; that one's manager;
high priority email and enlarge your man-
hood spam; battery chicken, leathered ham pie;
visions of efficiency and a potted peace
lily that I'll have to water next time;
workmates eroticising over calling it quits;
workmates swearing their colleagues are drooped shits;
squirly-whirlies on paper; the toilet floor *Star*;
a prissy carpark barrier blocking the car.

I saw it coming, loopy-go-lucky
muff-eared tongue-wagging happy-
as-sunlight mutt with scutched fawn coat:
a hop-skip-tittupping half-labrador
in a swagger chasing its own moist snout
filled with wonder, careening from sidepath
to roadway in a slavered rabbit dream,
leaving me two seconds to size up
I couldn't brake because the pimped-up
Micra up my ass was too near, too fast—
Dumph! It tail-chased its death throes in the wing-
mirror spinning, bad-moon howling

out of sight. I'd no end of time to stop
but never did as the Micra overtook me,
for I might have had to carry that hyper-
ventilating half-corpse or matted carcass
with fleas and nothing in its eyes
up some farmyard lane to a child or sour
culchie into *Deliverance*, and, anyway,
I wanted to get home to eat and channel-
surf for something decent or close my eyes
and drown in my sofa, so I hammered
headward down that road of sun and hay.

I va-va-voomed but the dog kept spinning
although left long behind, whirligigging
in a rear view of my mind so that I couldn't
avert my eyes from that spinning jenny
death-dervish below the sky churning
buttermilk, lobster, apricot and kale.
The flat road lined with moonwort demanded
I turn back—but then I'd have to confess
I'd gone on for thirteen miles under pricked pines
hounding me, making me want to shunt
up to race-speed and take-off past the police
lurched with speed guns behind the '30' sign.

I might have pulled over and left
my car's front doors flung openwide—
a hollow craft abandoned by picnic
tables in a litterblown parking bay
awaiting its lost passengers' return—
and hurled myself over the hedge to roam
google-eyed through deergrass and junipers
under a vanilla-rippled sky of crab shell,
tarragon and kelp, to find a runnel
flanked with bittercress and agrimony
where I'd lie and let the water-pepper
and salt-grass finger through me.

As I lay by the leak and lint of that runnel
with blaeberries and zigzag clover riddled
through me, under puma-skinned skies,
I might have looked over the mantilla
of sheaves, stooks and stubble strewn across
that landscape of labrador downs,
or rolled beneath a yew to catch its leaves
contrailed by cream-slathered clouds
over the dank earth turning round;
I might have lain below a fluttering of birds
filling my eye-bowls with nests of hay
by the gash of a distant carriageway.

I might have drifted off, crossed-over lanes
to collide in a slipstream of coming
and going, never here nor there but up
in the air, chasing homeward where to-do
lists are lurking, waiting for night to flip
my fried mind over until morning's
automatic return to the car and journey
back to join that withered fantail of online
satellite navigation and in-car 3D
lapdance simulation, along those pointillist
phone masts and sycamores still arching
the flat road's bore through sun-gilt and harvest.

When I finally steered and veered the bend
into Belfast and turned into my street,
I could have killed for a takeaway
but it was my turn to take the wee one's
fire engine, fluffy dog and laser gun
to bed where we lay below his globed atlas lamp,
self-timed to fade, rotating projected
continents on the borderlined walls'
night-blue planetarium, where we read
until drift-off into nothing, unmoored
from the axled turn and low-watt embers
of the earth's spinning top left long behind.

MORNING EMERGES OUT OF MUSIC

We dip, drop and dovetail in a cabaret
with crushed daiquiris and spellbound
maracas clippety-clapping the way
words click together and channel their sound
to a gorge-drop, a doorway, the sky-top's
blue veil. But then alarms ring, the music stops
and I wake to a fade-out, an aftersound
of bebble behind a curtain of air
that I chase through, my head dancing around
after rhythms without meaning, without care.

HARVEST

1

The two of them were forever banging
on about keeping your conscience spick and span
as a scoured kitchen surface and grafting
bone-hard in life's grim dockyard, each time giving
it everything. If a peeler took one through
the cummerbund outside the secret policeman's
dancehall, or Marks and Spencers blew
its windows one hundred and seventy-
five feet in the air to rain down arrows on the newly
disfigured, they'd be livid if I didn't wash my hands.

Maybe this is why I'm licking my chops
at the thought of microwaved trays
of pork bangers and bleached potato slops,
driving to Killymoon through hay fields and green
fields decked with pat-caked cows;
why my parents have turned into odd
truisms, viruses mutating through the thin streams
of my brain into screenplays of low-beamed
corners in dancehalls; why I'm wondering how
two free wills become two peas in a pod.

2

Half-baked under the spalding orange rays,
they birl and dunt their pitchforks in the fum.
A horse's scream of rain will soon come
and wash all this away, but now the women lay

the table with hot boxty bread. She sucks an orange finger.
His breeks are ripped to flitterjigs
as he snuffles his neb and spies the stoppled eaves
of her breasts, before gobbing a pure emerald yinger.

And he can't help but to think
of her in a bool of earth-swell, the hurt
weaver's kiss of her tights, raising her skirts
against the clay-baked orange-brown turf bink.

Now they trudge back along the oaten
shingle, a bunch of branny-faced boys in jouked
breeks by the reed-kissed bebble of a brook.
It's hard to judge when the sky will be opened.

Trigger-happy tomcats and hornets jet
into the sun, their motherloads dead set
on the clay-baked cities of Iraq, as I sit
back and order an overcooked frozen fillet
of salmon with hard potatoes and spoon-
mashed turnip with my parents at Killymoon's
nearest Hotel, my newborn son on my breast
with my Ma insisting, despite my cloud-dark frown,
that a brandy-soaked sugar cube is best
for traumatic nights as the rain knuckles down.

Someday I might return, and tell him this
is near where they met, where they might have been
married, as the rain batters remorseless
on watchtowers, their camouflaged polytetrafluoroethylene,
as I lead him down the road of falling
hazels and vetch, finger to finger
until he lets go and leaves me by a reed-shushing
brook under the sky's orange plumes,
the fallout winds and elder
stealing kisses on the road to Killymoon.

DEATH BY PREVENTABLE POVERTY

Three seconds passed, another one dead,
I walked past violets and wind-flowers,
cowbind, eglantine, moonlight-coloured may
and ivy serpentine snaking as I railed
after the epiphanies were over,
reeled among white cups and clover,
flag flowers, riverbuds awaiting the hail
that will hail on oxslips, bluebells looking to stay
the west-blown cyclone, these galled hours
and phantoms, children, flustered in my head,
yellow, and black, and pale, and red.

LAGANSIDE

I cannot call back the time, lasso the millions
of minutes by the scruff of their scrawny
wee seconds, or knockout the lost years,
bop the back of their heads and bale
them into a getaway van that will welly-it
to a warehouse where time is put right
by a crack team of agents in tandem
with a renegade but brilliant neurobiologist.
No, the missing months are truly missing,
marooned, cut adrift, left for bye-bye to dry
out in the wreck of themselves, then stalk
an undead and hollow land forever thirsting.

Anyway, it's been ages since I last happened
by this riverside walkway, where the dead
wood reeked by weather's spring cleaned.
And I never learned the name of anything,
but it's nice to see no-one's ripped the plants
out by their roots and burnt and pissed over
the empty burned space where the ripped-up,
pissed-on plants used to be. And it really is
great to stick-on names that you've heard
to whatever you like without caring. So,
along this riverside pathway that snakes
through the city, this laminate lagoon,

buckeyes and rose of Sharon bushes occupy
snowberry banks, restharrow and gillyflowers
garland bamboo trunks and sapodillas,
while a lotusbird perches to coo-coo
with currawongs and chuck-will's-widows,
orangequits and greenshanks tra-la twittering,
tittering and tottering on high branches
of lacquer trees, getting liquored on ylang
ylang, oakmoss, dragon's blood and thyme.
But tiring of this, I ask my better half
if she knows what anything is, and she quotes to me:
'Happiness is good health and bad memory'.

A man screams. I jitter. But he's shouting
at his pupils tinned in a pointy-headed
rowboat, and I'm almost insulted,
given the streets are full of men who would
think nothing of going right up to a tiger
lily and scrunching its corolla, who'd shoot
the crows for target practice if they could take out
their guns; and so, I shouldn't exaggerate,
given that if a duck even tried to quack-
quack in that water, it would be a stone-
dead duck before long; given that beneath
the bokey fudged mulch you can see 3D

nightmares of chains and pulleys, high school
bullies, trolleys, satanic creepy crawlies,
a Black & Decker angle grinder, outstanding
debt reminders, buckled pushchairs, threadbare
pink and olive striped deckchairs, moustachioed
schoolmasters, startled newscasters introducing
shots of headshots, roadblocks, deadlocks,
English cocks and Irish Jocks, mutilated livestock,
a timer's tick-tock, confused with the cistern's drip-
drop, keeping you up to panic at a midnight knock-
knock, which is just a drunk neighbour who thought
is missus must ive change da fuckin front-dure lock.

Anyway, while all this flows towards Belfast Lough,
it's not exactly Xanadu above water either,
not quite Honolulu, when above and beyond
the trees all I can see are weed-nooked rustyards
fighting for space with erect hotels and pearly
office centres, tall cranes stalking everywhere:
tower cranes, hydraulic cranes, cranes for all terrain
policing thin streets in bright-sprayed armatures,
lording it over buildings like a supreme new race,
looking towards their unused elders hung
in sorrow in the dockyards to the east; whether
in sympathy, or saying up yours, I'm not sure.

Closer to the riverside, terraced doors keep
their mouths shut and children are clamped
in by barricade from this steep fall of river-
bank and clean public walkway, though buttered
faces size me up from behind a useless wall,
cursing the river's limitations, my trespass,
this tourist sprawl. But then, moving onward,
by a cream call centre, a sunbed-skinned sales team
have finished their shift and stream through
the fence-gate to traipse toward happy hour
promotions, black power retro-nights, their navel
studs and highlights sparked by waterlight.

But these airs, this river, these sights have not
been to me some happy-clappy totem,
nor a masochistic home-truth tucked away
in the dark corner of my room mid the nee-
nar drone or bling-bling neon of foreign
towns and cities where I've ordered Pad
Thai noodles and drawn the blinds to dwell
on the blank page at the end of 'Ovid
in Tomis'. It's just I've never come down
since these tracks were laid, and this path
is like my tongue after biting a Pink Lady
cling-wrapped in a thin film of cellophane.

Of course, this happens all the time: you walk
up to your neighbour and note his nostril
hairs, dimples, pocks, scars, cheeks and creviced
chin; then five minutes later you catch his nut
brown eyes in the light and all the features
of his face fuse into something whole but shifting
like this river; or you run your hardly-haired
fingers over the deep blue tiles that line your bath
and soon they're pigeon's neck or tortoiseshell,
turquoise flashing eyes on a peacock's wing;
so it's unsurprising I'm a bit bamboozled
by this crash and build of trees and concrete

under ice-blue skies, which are hardly ice-
blue, but electric, kingfisher, and air-force
blue stretched over this crocodilic river
preying straight for the lough's open maw
to leave behind all guarantees; horse chestnuts
and hazel trees; the roadways' injured circuitry;
wheelie-bins and empties; wideboys hawking
blow to the gothic daughters of the haute
bourgeoisie; and my better half and me
below clouds that taper the city's spires,
cupolas, scaffolding, lithe birds of origami.

No wonder I'm astray, a little bit this way
and that way, for the dockyards and ghettoes
look like a grey-quiffed and tattooed uncle
intensely line dancing on a hot night-
club floor, thinking he might yet score,
like I've been caught with my guard down
by this dizzy glint and easy rapture
of poplar and clover, wire-fence and river
flooding towards the basin's broken jaws
as if hit-and-running from a crime scene,
though flushed and peach-blushed with pleasure
at the prospect of coming to a head,

having it out for once and forever
as the missing months and years dredge
past the massage of washed-out slogans,
sleek towers, ghosted union buildings,
the river overrunning its own ledge
to find itself played out in a final flush
into open seas, under drizzled rain,
while the sky arrests an outbound plane,
and my better half lags behind to savour
the shifting terrain, leaving me to find
our way back to the streets, knowing
I'll never leave here, or come back again.

ELOQUENCE

Who would not speak, in their quieter fancies,
as a gannet coasts the blue—to rise, halt
without breaking wing, and kamikaze
downward at breakneck speed, break the salt
water surface, plunge with dead-eyed accuracy
the ice-shock deep, then splash to resurface
with a glittered life writhing in the beak?
Who would not lip such a sentence?
So I would wind myself up to a peak,
lift off from the plains, then relax
and stretch out to soar, dip and turn,
but there'd be some dark slick of pitch to tax
such flight, and I'd splutter, coast-bound and waxed
with the tar-and-gicked feathers of a rigid tern.

THE DEBT COLLECTOR

Between the anticipation and aftermath,
the trickle of water and quenching of thirst,
between the wish and what comes out in the wash,
the seed packet and gladioli bloom,
between now, then and when,
all you know will vanish down the plug hole.

No matter how ripe the fruit in the bowl,
erotic the violets, erratic the stars,
at night empty rooms gather you in their claws.
Their silence licks you. All that is lost,
all that is botched streams into one strange image
in the mirror and wears your eyes.

Darker by the day, you feel a stranger
hover at the window, eavesdrop on your calls,
at your shoulder in darkened corridors,
head-bowed two seats ahead of you on the bus,
in the shade of the lindens and silver limes,
adept and ready, wearing white gloves.

On a bare wall the clock-face ticks.
That you were never liable is a myth
like easy money. So live accordingly.

The hours are long, the months disappear,
and the moment nears when he will come.
He will speak with your voice.

Only if you're lucky will he come without hurt,
steal into your borrowed home
and lead you through this town's coil
of limbs and longing, bear you through the rain,
along nameless roads to a green wood
whose river weaves its murmur with conifer song.

There he'll lay you down in the riverweed,
clubmoss, hazel scrub, witch butter,
covered in a shallow night of crawling soil.
So make the most of your loan, though all that
is gone, or is going, will never let you go.
In our deaths our debt will grow.

IN THE SHADOW OF THE MOURNES

The wind gowled at windows, howled through hedgerows,
    uprooted a dead-rooted tree;
the full moon looked like a full moon does
    in a Hammer Horror DVD;
the road was a scar on the curving neck
    of high heathered fell and drumlin;
        and Johnny Black came driving,
        gear-grinding, jack-knifing,
Johnny Black was soon arriving
    at The Devil's Coach Road Inn.

He wore a Hugo Boss leather jacket
    and tight cream Diesel jeans,
his Dolce & Gabbanna t-shirt was a v-
    necked peppermint green.
He wore Converse shoes, ribbed Calvin Klein whips,
    dangled a Camel between his lips,
        and he drove a Beemer,
    a jet-black gleamer,
a five-gear screamer with maximum bling that he'd fling
    from nought to ninety in a blip.

It was 3:30am, the bar was shut, he parked
        fifty yards down the road.
The wind whammed into a corrugated shed
        so you'd think it about to explode,
yet he sallied like an alley cat to the back-
        yard door, and who was waiting there,
            but the owner's daughter
        Kylie with raven-black mascara
smudged by rainwater running down the eaves,
        down through her raven-black hair.

Now Kylie was married and only helped
        her Da pour the Guinness
when her husband, Danny White,
        went away on business.
But his business wasn't kosher, it was Columbian.
        He had the run of every local town.
            You didn't screw
        with Danny, everybody knew
you'd be worse off than black and blue:
        the most murderous misdemeanant in South Down.

Danny had his doubts and had Mad Dog Frank
        spy on Kylie, to fish for anything fishy,
staked out on a hill with his pit bull Francis
        in a beat-up brown Mitsubishi
to report on any ballyhoo. So Mad Dog Frank was slobbering

over his usual stakeout dreams,
  when the pit bull
Francis pulled and drooled
at you-know-who, wrenching Frank from the willow-switch
  and snatch of his Hungarian whiplash Queen.

'Hang in tight, sugar doodle. Don't worry, I'm on
  for a windfall tonight.
I'll be back at five, and then we'll take off on
  the first Magaluf-bound flight.'
Johnny kissed her wet mouth, her lush curving neck,
  thinking he was clever.
    Back in his car he zipped
  off lickety-split
like a bullwhip and ripped straight for Danny's hush-hush
  coke deal outside Rostrevor.

Mad Dog Frank pushed Francis the pit bull away.
  He was starting to feel the stress.
He thought of Kylie's hips and curving haunches in her soft
  long sapphire split-leg dress,
her flaming lips, ravines of raven-black hair
  and the snow-white avalanche
    of her breasts.
  Yes, in his best
dreams he'd nest smug and snuggle there forever.
  Mad Dog Frank was Special Branch.

He'd worked undercover for five years, starting in Belfast,
    then Newry city
on small-time deals using Francis the pit bull
    for don't-fuck-around authenticity.
Now in a top crew, knowing what Danny could do
    with any old kitchen knife,
        he was on the brink,
    about to sink
him but all he could think of was the avalanching sapphires
    of his flame-lipped and rainwater-hipped wife.

Mad Dog Frank guessed green-eyed Danny had lost the plot
    · with his paranoid suspicions of Kylie
and ignored him, hoping for a flash of her flesh-coloured tights
    when she reached up for the expensive brandy.
Now he rubbed the big O of each eye, thinking it over.
    Johnny Black? Who would ever
        have guessed? But he thought it best
    to act fast and get the arrest
now lest Danny shot or strangled or stubbed her:
    so he called in the deal near Rostrevor.

Danny White was cold and hard,
    Johnny Black, all heat and bluster.
Black was barely twenty-one, White was old school,
    ex-quartermaster.
White was careful, Black was hasty,

the two together would surely be tasty.
    White had courted Kylie
  for five years while he built a tidy
ceasefire operation. She'd straddled Black within an hour
  in the back of a blue A4 Audi.

At 4:14 a Special Unit moved in on Danny
  and his dealers.
At 4:18 Johnny was too cooked to take mark
  of all the peelers'
unmarked cars, and burst in thinking this was *Heat*
  and he was Al Pacino.
    He fired a shot
  from his sawn-off shot-
gun and promptly took one in the head, while Danny was riddled,
  acting like Robert De Niro.

Seven years on, Frank works in Liverpool and sleeps,
  if he sleeps, in his car,
off his face on dirty money, pimping immigrants,
  throwing big tips at bright tits in a Hooters bar.
Monthly he pays for humiliation and the willow-switch
  of a heroin-eyed Hungarian whore,
    haunted by shrivelled wreaths,
  shovelled knees and knuckled teeth
grovelling under broken noses, grot and snatters
  on a raven-black Carrickfergus shore.

He thinks of red-diesel runs under spilt-milk skies,
    debt collections in ice-bound caravans,
Mickey Finns and schoolgirls, ringed pit bull fights,
    migrant worker scams,
camouflaging stashes in ramshackle barns
    with sheep bleating, abattoired and ardent.
      He thinks of Kylie in Magaluf
    with her Polish chef
under the thatched roof of her Irish tapas bar
    and adjacent beachfront apartment.

Sunsets, Zombies, Screwdrivers, Sours,
    Harvey Wallbangers, PG tips tea:
she still provokes a polka, serving vodka and cola
    while men still leer with shit-faced subtlety.
She thinks of her hard working Da
    and her long dead Ma who lies
      in the shadow of The Mournes
    under bent firs and whitethorn
as the soft air teases a crinkled smile below her wrinkled
    snow-white nose in the sunrise.

But at night she thinks of 5:00am, when the wind bawled
    in addiction and grief;
when dirty Frank emptied himself of the ambush,
    Danny's money, his own raw heat on his knees;

when the road was a scar on the curving neck
    of high heathered fell and drumlin,
        and Mad Dog came driving,
    blind-riding, soon colliding
through the raven-black rain, under an unreal moon,
    into The Devil's Coach Road Inn.

FROM IN WHOSE BLENT AIR
ALL OUR COMPULSIONS MEET

Put your clothes on, she said, you're not dead
yet and we must take the air, and so on.
Yah de yah de yah. And so, we take the air.
When summer nettles with sunblaze and pollen,
when birdsong crackles like a salesman's cold call,
when fizz-fuzzed may bugs bizz-buzz (blah blah blah),
when we've gone to seed, sickened by our sequel—
falling fruit in the laughing livid air—
it's time to *do-re-mi* through the day's *fa-so-la-ti*,
its music of movement, scored by shadows.
No car, nor bike, nor bus, but one
foot following the other to a field or wood-
land as the town disappears, to conclude
where sycamore leaves shiver in the sun.

How the mind drifts, as we mosey along
through brief nights and long walks in public
parks or by shorelines, by the riverside's
crinkled ferns and fronds, traipsing past
hawksbeard and hawthorn, the brambled
hedge-banks of the cindertrack; how the mind,
as the melony sunblaze spangs bangles
over windlebrooke and witch-hazel that waggles
and sways while the breeze blows wild garlic
and you pull your hair back to the music
of the moment; how the mind plays away
and other times and places take shape and surface,
fuse and fester in your mind's shifting frame
you chase through again, and again, and again.

We walk, and our legs tick-tock toward fire,
or that rift in the ground where dusted lilacs
and wild teasel are growing among windblown
cellophane, used Featherlites, discount flyers;
and still we put our best foot forward
to trek our winding cindertrack under blue-red
sweeps over dead heathered hills, by a high-walled
trinity of partly-scrubbed street slogans that show:
'Vote for Sin', 'Fuck the Pop', 'God is Go'.
Later in the dusk, we'll crash and tune in
to the drone of our head's hive and honeycomb
of sun-gilt and dark evaporation.
Sometimes it doesn't help knowing
there is more than one way of going.

Going for a pop song, going to pot
in a Homebase bed of jasmine and bergamot:
when you reach over, and your shadow spews
over my bent of mind, I want to do with you
what darkness does with candlelight,
what an egg whisk does with an egg white,
what the blazes of sunlight do with the sycamore,
what a well-oiled hinge does with a back door,
what a whetstone does with a Kobayashi knife,
what the postman's second ring does for a flagitious wife,
what Castrol GTX Magnatec oil does with a V8 engine,
what the wind does with wrens high on a buffet and whim as they spiral
    and swoop and hover and spin;
then you reach over, your eyes pursed and finite,
and blow out the candle. Here comes the night.

In the morning we wake and board the bus
packed like a waiting room for a passport
or injection, then pass into our grave
and buckled grid of concrete and bustled
compartmentalisation and feel the eyes
of silent police within the workplace,
the long arms of check-outs that cordon
each store, bars clamping alarmed doors
against dirty sneakers with Burger King beakers.
In some such way, we dreep through the day
as the hours wind down. We talk for minutes,
then go under to our dreams' self-harm
to haggle with the quick and the dead,
the wards of night, waiting for the alarm.

Dreaming of murder, dreaming of kites,
dreaming of leather that fits good and tight,
of thighs and hot tongues from morning to night;
dreaming of widgets, of television,
dreaming of first place in a competition;
dreaming of Havana, of counter-intelligence,
enormous mojitos, a forbidden entrance;
dreaming of fire and sword upon parched veldt,
rain-swept gorse, shattered windows, shattered delft;
dreaming of a trophy wife and hyperbolical wealth,
a peachy brand new brand name blushing on the shelf;
dreaming of hawks, dreaming of doves:
between the weird filth below, blasted wonder above,
dreaming a sentence in the cells of love.

My love is a mansion with many rooms to see.
I'm asbestos.
My love's a glittering surface, scrubbed spotlessly.
I'm the germ that can withstand Domestos.
My love's a Penelope rose. I'm the canker.
My love is Independence. I'm the Union.
My love is a passenger and I'm the wanker
sat next to her, eating egg and onion
sandwiches, saying 'I'm no right-winger, but . . .'
My love is a peach. I'm its hard nut.
My love's an open threshold. I'm the dark within the door.
My love is untouched land. I'm a shovel. Go dig.
My love's a high-minded principle. I'm its war.
Come to think of it, my love is a prig.

We take the air, it has no surface, it has no depth;
but the air won't cease to put another crease
upon your changing face, in the corner
of your eye. As our slow path turns to dewed grass
and the pixel-rich sky thrums, we reach our tree
while an aeroplane cuts the mustard of the sun
in the song-stained air. With mayflies jigging:
this is your life. May bugs buzzing: no real
harm done. Ferns and leaves dancing. And your dress
is burnt sienna, you breathe the shade's perfume;
a wren breaks free, your face lights up—a may-apple
in bloom, or an open book. With shadows twitching:
look, everything's moving. Raw earth turning:
you're not dead yet. The livid air laughing.

DOWN THROUGH DARK
AND EMPTYING STREETS

Open a new window.
Go on and Google yourself.
Open Facebook and update
all trace of yourself.

While you search MySpace,
sync your apps, correct a wiki,
blah blah on your blog,
tweet and stream, you see

such-and-such has got in touch,
requesting you as a Facebook friend.
And the name's slow-dawned gravity
widens the window, weirds and sends

you plunging into the déjà-vu
of a phlegm-skied twilight
with unreal soldiers on the walls
lit by fire-red and air-blue streetlights;

sends you trampling through the fank
and crumble and Regal packets
of your hedgeless estate
in a tarnished and tufty leather jacket,

flappered and frazzled paisley shirt,
scuffed and shagged-out oxblood boots,
walking away from your mother, the screech
of your sister's wee black flute,

past the clanking monkey bars,
swings and roundabout of a dog-dark
dungeon of a playground,
through a sinister elm-guarded car park,

cutting to the main street through
the grounds of a windowless factory,
past the pock-marked and *Jesus Lives*
walls of the public library

while the sky turns to liquorice,
dull cardigan and tobacco fumes
embered with persimmon blushes,
melon-flowers, mango blooms;

walking until you catch a hint
of her toe-to-heel click-clack
and follow her past scuppled shops,
dead-end alleys, hokey flats;

past head-the-ball hardnuts driving by
in souped-up Cortinas and Capris
hunting their prey; and she's driving you
doolally, knocked at the knees

as you follow her past the bookies'
arcade machines and nudgers'
Fisher Price lights and beep-bop-bings;
past the queue of scratching pudgers

in the chip shop where a pouty girl
shovels cod with a lizard-eye
love bite, Princess Diana pendant
and powdered-over black eye;

past chain-smoking bars with ducktape
on the cracks of their panes
silhouetted by the awful size
and dormant metal of dockyard cranes;

and you're all hearts and flowers
with each step into the square,
where she turns so you can finger
her pampas bleached and hair-

sprayed hair, and she says Hey there,
in her clown voice, is that a spanner
in yer works? under the twenty-foot
high frown of an *Ulster Says No* banner

and her rib-cage is delicate white
as flour on a fillet of fish
while her lips, still hot with sausage,
salt and malt vinegar, mouth a wish

and clarty newspapers carry news
of the weekend's nil-nils
windblown with Special Brew
cans and Styrofoam cups as you thrill

to her octopus fingers,
the probe and prod of her plum of a tongue,
your teeth and her teeth tapping together,
holding breath until kingdom come.

She asks will all this last forever?
against the dun Woolworth's door.
Now your hard drive hums and haws.
You waver between *Confirm* and *Ignore*.

IN THESE AISLES

From an ASBO to Asda
I've come a long way, they say,
as if stacking shelves was a
big dream of mine, like 'whey-hey
it's Spreads and fucken Preserves today',
although it would, in fact, be okay

so far as such shit goes, I suppose,
if it wasn't for the likes of her
with her coriander and nose
in the air, her sun-tinted spikes of hair,
crashing into me like some charioteer,
like the fact I'm simply standing here

working my gonads off is some grave
insult, like it's big of her to brave
these rough aisles—some muckamuck
with a River Cottage cookbook
who most likely has a big fuck
you car and two kids she never looks

at but is always idolising
(crooked teeth, front of the school choir)
with some accessorized husband most aroused
when fantasising about finalising
with online buyers bidding higher and higher,
for all of her low-buttoned blouse,

her fuck me pink push-up bra,
her trimmed asparagus and Laksa
paste and vermin-fucken-celli
noodles and the silken jelly
of her soft, floating, flower-skirted arse.
For me to even dream of her's a farce

but she'll see. For I'm going to have
me a big black Audi with satnav
and leather seats, and I'll burn past her
and every single fucken manager
in this place. I won't be down because of her,
or them. Not even my liaison officer.

He followed me once, got on my bus—
like I wouldn't clock a mumpsimus
with a file chart slitching after me—
so I took him to The Winds where the peelers
won't go, and left him outside Digsy's
front door (and Digsy takes no prisoners)

while I sleeched out the back of the house
to call at Britney's for a bong and tea.
For the next month he couldn't look at me
without his smush turning rufous,
and then he was replaced. Fucken doofus.
I'll show the lot of them. Now, 1, 2, 3 ...

I'm the safe pair of hands they want me to be,
stacking Poptarts, Branflakes, muesli,
Rice Crispies, Sugar Puffs, Cocopops,
Crunchy Nut Cornflakes in the King of Shops.
But when I've shelved the Frosties and Weetabix,
I take my pay, I get my kicks ...

LOOKING FORWARD TO LEAVE

There were sliced-beef brown-bread triangles,
boys on one side, girls on the other side,
hair claws, white socks, rashed necks strangled
by tight top buttons and crooked ties,
beakers of dull orange that dirty Chris gargled
before nudging: *which one ye goanna ride?*
And when I tried to learn to dance for you
my fingers marked your forearms red and blue.

Then there were blue coats on one side, red coats
on the other side, a battle of the bands,
banners waving in the sun, black flutes, eight-carat-
gold signet rings, a line drawn in the sand,
balmorals, plumes and epaulets, taunts and gloats
over hard-drilled drums. And when I raised my hand
to fight for you, my eye flamed hot flamingo
pink then gloamed to a stoned avocado.

But on Basra's streets there are no clear sides,
just dust and heat-hazed aftershocks, infrared
sensor systems, suspect cars we've pulled aside—
you'd think their eyes would pop from their heads
once they've eyed me; although I'm mostly inside
the Warrior, or in barracks with hotheads
blasting hardcore beats that would drill your head:
hole in your head, in your mutherfucking head.

We move north to what they all call *the shit*
tomorrow and I'm unsure when I'll next return
to your emails without the entire unit
looking over either side of me at the screen,
but I'll be keeping a diary, to write it
all down, each dream in which I burn
to song-flames, poppies and embers,
leaves we might walk through this November

when the leaves, flared to fire-colour, take leave,
fall into memory; for there is a book
of books we all carry inside, its leaves
crisply turning, and I remember that look
in your eyes when, before I left, you laughed—
there's magic in the music and the music
is in us—I read in that look for some such
meaning, in this desert, my make-up smutched.

Another unmarried woman with a child
has been taken, beheaded, purified;
and I live for my leave, when I'll slide what you called
my un-be-fucking-lieve-able legs either side
of you. I look forward to nothing but the cold,
cans of Harp and soda farls, my hair newly dyed,
the soft skirt I'll wear, the music we'll play,
and we'll get hammered on Remembrance Day.

Let me flee tick-tock time's paralysis
and float through unplumbed time's pure dead
brilliant book (not like a book when being read,
but like afterwards, when it swims in your head)
of interconnections. The clock looks so sad
because it always knows what time it is;

yet if time ticks on, let me not wallow
but face the facts, which cluster and collide from
one moment to the next, but never join
together as I toss small coins
at a homeless woman, and the next one,
then walk past the rest in a sham of shadows,

silhouettes, shopfronts, lampposts, car lights
leering like fluorescent chrysanthemums;
past the bobbling torchlights of mobile phones,
warm flat windows, third floor homes,
illuminated cyclists and the white wan
moon-holes on the thigh of a drunk girl's tights.

THE GREEN ROSE

Hell won't be full till you're in it,
she said, ye lazy scut, ye big sour-faced
whipster; and in a huff he hoofed it
down the rise, past the stream, thunder-faced
past bogbane, water-violet and marsh-marigolds,
cress and sorrel spread over the surface
of the stream, effing and blinding as he rolled
with spilling fingers soft Virginian shag—
sucked in deep, blew out slow—and strolled
past blackthorn, barley fields and clay-
crusted hills, where he lay down among white
butterflies, ragweed, dandelions, clags
on a grass bed, green-waved in sunlight,
the wings of crows brooming shadows upon it.

Bright light sprawling white cotton clouds
looked like they'd never heard of rain:
some saw in them maps, memory shapes,
continents, faces of demons, gondolas
lazing through sunstreams. He saw sheep
grazing in a greener-than-green field
bedizzled by buttercups carpeted down
to a fizzing hedge, stone path and two
apple trees standing sentry to a view
of the lough, coastline, chopped open sea,
oblivious to things that might have been
or might be, passing lives, the mist and creep
of stolen thoughts, the dead and unborn
drifting, on their backs, counting sheep.

Howl on to your horses for the death of sweet
Jesus, he almost said, almost overpowered,
sensing her sniping behind him, the sweetmeat
stains of her apron caked in buttermilk and flour,
mouth tight shut as a crow's arse, while she looked
down on his backside, his head in the flowers,
where he'd seen a green bloom that he mistook
for a rose for a moment. Once she'd groused and grutched
back indoors he snuck to the barn and took
out the clippers to snick around the edge
of the house, but she stooked her head out
and blared: don't make a big barney balls of that hedge!
then went back to griddling hot potato bread
asking where's his mind? what is his head?

He dreamed she was a cloud, frayed at the seams,
bits of her floating hither, others thither,
edges wisped, funnelled, whispered and curled,
tentacles feeling for the way the four winds
were blowing. In the evening she would turn
hyacinth, rose, japonica and orange
blossom on a flasket of lemon and blue.
On her best days a big hole would open
in her head and a stairway to marvels
might spotlight through. But mostly she'd be
degged grey, gathering her bits together
in a bloated, grimaced, grave-bellied swell
fit to split open a black harvest of grain,
head-hung children who would forbear her rain.

Clegged boots by the door, heavy hair dredged,
battered and bowed by the gravel-hard rain,
sullen and speechless, swilling the dregs
of his tea, she thought him feck-brained,
his head on the table, engrossed with weevils
creeping over fried crumbs and egg-stains
on his thick clacked plate. Why in the name
of the devil's good Da did you go and do a daft
thing like that? she asked, once she'd weaselled
that he'd signed on the straight line of his draft
papers to leave her to the dootering cows—
to leave in his wake a trail of boot-shaped rifts
in the ground: sumped and tumid shrouds
of silt and glit, with his head in the clouds.

After he died in July nineteen-sixteen
she received this letter: *Dear Rosie,*
when I get a minute, here and there, I've been
rooted in Leaves of Grass, *which helps me see*
the sweet bay, bluebells and primrose-decked
tumps of our home. I hope you're not lonely.
I dreamt we were lying in a slaking field
edged with yellow-bloomed whin and green
flowers. I think they were roses. You pricked
your pink finger on one and as we leaned
back to watch the clouds you gave it to me
and I kissed it until the gash had been cleaned
among the high rushes of whispering barley.
Regards, with deepest love and sincerity.

When next July came she rose to head
out by the whitethorn and poplars, over tinder,
dogwood, docken-strewn paths, while overhead
she could see that white clouds were seething,
furious with ice, shape-shifters, mind-benders,
cheating forms sucking up something from nothing,
sailing over nettles, lungwort and thyme;
and she halted where the stream became a river
by the big elm: among buddleia and woodbine
she took off her blouse, checking nobody
was about, slipped from her skirts, and lowered
herself between two moss-bearded boulders
to flense and flush her still-young body
in the on-gush and go of breaking water.

Maybe he dreamed of Lady Dixon Park
or Clandeboye, maybe Killynether,
retreading leaves of grass, stooping to pick
wild tulips, bell heather, thinking 'There will never
be any more heaven or hell than there is now',
watching a felt-pelted bumble bee hover
in circles over a green flower that was new
to him, that was maybe a rose, as he grappled
with the long and the short of it. 'And I know
the amplitude of time' and other unforeseeable
lines swooped and made him think someone stooped
to pluck and blow him through the four winds; that maybe
'I am not contained between my hat and my boots',
no more than the green rose by hip, pricks or loveroot.

ON A COLD EVENING IN EDINBURGH

Night falls, as night will,
    out of nowhere and sprawls
black in the thick folds
    and pooled gloom
of itself, and crawls
    into every nook and cranny,
and frost will soon

crackle and slip over the surface
    of things, slick over thoroughfares
and alleyways, paves, cobbles
    and graves, while small moons
of satellites, passenger flights
    and haulage flights patrol
each and every square

inch of the hard-starred
    and static sky like pinhead
toxic blips that scour
    the dark, scar the air.
Fast cats eat the dead
    birds and foxes
rifle through recycling bins

while a bull-necked
    baby bawls and hauls
a breast of milk from bed
        and children dream of guns
and horses against the silhouette
    of hills in the distance.
On a night like this,

it's easy to forget little
    we can do or say is likely to avert
fingernails being torn from fingers,
        murder by hunger, genetic malice,
fuel terror that will tear the fatal earth.
    But there can be no turning
our backs on a world that's always turning

to tomorrow's open promise:
    maybe a quick death, maybe slow.
We may never know
        more than the lovesick and pierced teen
who lips blue smoke in an upward
    spiral from her bedroom window
raising wolf whistles from the street below,

but notice how people, like words,
    ache to attach themselves,
unload their burden, tingle and tie,

fuse and flow into a music
that can only be heard
   in gentle dreams.
Like books on bookshelves we lie

packed into terraces and towerblocks,
   bedsits and bungalows,
listening to passenger trains
     and haulage trains snuffle and cry
in the distance
   bearing untold and heavy cargoes
into the terror and solace of silence

or, for all we know,
   Hull, Bristol, Dover,
to set sail for greater islands
     where the occupied already turn over
to embrace a breeze-kissed
   morning and brace themselves
against the violence

without, the violence within.
   On a night like this,
little we can say or do is likely to call
     down the angels,
make the all mighty
   change their minds and suddenly
dedicate their lives to the bliss

of their wives of many long years.
　　But to simply cave in
when tomorrow crawls,
　　　　as tomorrow will, out of nowhere,
and slowly lose all trace
　　of ourselves; to give up the ghost,
let ourselves fall

and all but drop off the face
　　of the earth would be to follow
in the footsteps of the family
　　　　man who flees his family in the face
of the air-strike to save
　　his own skin, to break free
and sink or swim

in the edgeless desert and dead time
　　of himself; it would be
never to enter the true city;
　　　　never to put our bodies in the line
of ringless fingers, the winds
　　of change, their piercing slipstream;
never to crack open our lovesick

and spinning minds
　　to feel the solace and bliss
of these streets where we wake to dream,

dream to wake. On a night like this,
it's as if we haven't seen
    them all before: the hurt and the hurtful,
the hunted and unmissed;

legless couples locked together
    singing long dawn songs;
singles who've almost
        given up hoping to throw
their arms around anything but lipless
    visions amid sirens and engines;
the flickering ghosts

of flat screens through windows;
    the widows of the night;
raw girls in tartan minis and tight
        t-shirts under lamp posts;
the breeze and litter's side-street skirl;
    the recently bereaved taking flight,
breaking free in the back of a black taxi

racing past slumpers and stragglers
    ranting, raving, fumbling for a light;
past haulage trains and passenger planes
    breaching the limits of the city
bearing untold and heavy cargoes
    from Taipei, Mumbai, Beijing:
all lovers and loners, watchers

and wardens, captive and free,
    waiting for dark skies to crack
open onto what will be.
       This is what we know.
On a night like this,
    the world, the poem, is a ring.
Move like a butterfly, and sting.

APPROACHING YOUR TWO THOUSAND THREE HUNDRED AND THIRTY-THIRD NIGHT

The dusk drapes its fug, weighs on your mind
in the back seat, wound up by what you can't see
as we wind through this darkened braid of streets.
Headlights will do what they can to help find
our way home, while you shuffle and mutter,
your head with the stars, questions that repeat
but hove unanswered in the creeping sea
of night. I'd say you're right: whatever's the matter
in us might well be the same matter in the sun,
each ear of corn, grain of rice, granule of sand;
in humpback whales fluking to sing the depths
of the ocean; and the ocean, and zebras,
and bluebells, and woodswallows; and perhaps,
little head, tired arms, also the moon.

When tomorrow comes remember your why? why? why?
and we'll begin with shorelines where gulls arch
consonants in the great vowel of the sky.
We'll walk the city, and woods, where we'll dwell on
dewdripped spiderwebs in the sun, sprunted larches,
couples with dogs poop-scooping on the green,
tall nettles and deep coombs; so when the dark
comes you'll have bearings with which to explore
witches' covens, hard words, war zones, famines,
dragonheads, and the cruel laughter that bores
into your mind. This is what the night is for,
little head, speedy mind. When tomorrow comes
we'll take in what we can from town and park.
Together we will walk through the common.

Now that night lets fall her black hair
and watches over you, wraps you in her shawl,
the day drains from you like water from sand
to leave grains of memory, sifting on the shore
of your mind. Such sands of time may fall
through your fingers, sting your eyes, fly everywhere.
But little head, tired arms, try not to dwell on
dead-eyed meanness, why the world is unfair.
I'd say in our dreamtime we woke on an island,
all of us, where there was plenty for all,
but one had a machine gun and made everyone
else slave to the bone for their thrupenny share
while he sat laughing, eating melons,
coining cruel names, fingering his weapon.

Little head, tired arms, speedy mind,
let yourself flow with the thrum of the engine.
Driving through the warpled night we can find
our way home, and then worry about heaven.
If there is a heaven it is chained to the earth
like flight to the air, a mirror to light,
air to the ground, rigor mortis to birth.
And if you could look down from the height
of heaven you would see us as loose grains
of rice, or sand, scattered and small
crisscrossed scars on the face of the earth.
We've been sifted through an impassable wall
we will pass through twice. That is all.
You ask what we are for? I'd say imagine.

WHISKEY

Listen for the whist of unrippled wells
of water, still ponds, dead quiet lakes
you might walk to through wheatfields
and rolled fields of new-flowered flax
into an otherworld of woodland

where boys have stopped playing
soldiers and laid down broken branches
to finger caterpillars, where you might
first have opened lips to feel a tongue
alive in your mouth moons ago.

Lie still by such a low pond and catch
the thistled breeze and shallow flies,
insects twitching in the verbena
and firethorn, the tufted clouds'
degression, a distant Citroën engine.

Better still, go on a winter's night
when you might catch the chattered tink
of your own teeth, the buffets of a barn
owl's wings, shadows that flusker and flitch
over the silver pool's ice and secrets.

For the days are taken and poured
like whiskey into the well of a glass:
for a while we hold the sunset
in hard-worked hands, then drain the glass.
Look through the window on a winter's

night—some might possess your body
but none the hole vented through
that two-way glass, no more than hold
the snow, the lunatic, the vanishing child,
as you lose your reflection in the frost.

For we are swept up in the city's
cashflows and contusions, violet mouths
and japing eyes, until one night,
land-locked in our poverty, caught and cut
up by the glaze of cold eyes, we feel

a sliver of still water, a midnight pool,
and in that fleet stretch of time
before we empty our rusting spirits
into the well of a glass, deep within us,
broken cubes of moonlight tinkle and chime.

FROM **HERE COMES THE NIGHT**

Wanting to write a note perfect for you,
I was zonked by ten minutes to midnight
and gave up the ghost. So I scribbled blue
nothings on the sheer face of the white,
scrunched it to all but the shape of a ball and threw
it to my darkgreen fuzz of unclean carpet,
putting on a self-circling sad sung song
of lost days instead, cursing my tongue.

I heard a tin can trickle down empty streets.
I heard televisions flick themselves on in vacant rooms.
I heard a telephone's *dring-dring* repeat, and repeat.
I heard a door-hinge creak, then suddenly, a slammed boom.
I heard lonely computers receive a tweet.
I heard a CD stick at *Blue … Blue … Blue*, never reaching the moon.
I heard a clock's tick-tock-tick turn *dong … dong … dong*
and something changed in the air, something wrong.

I awoke and the room was in disfigured shape.
The desk sweated. Walls grew hair. Sour curtains
sipped the night with wrinkled lips. My clothes in a heap
looked a dead man's, while the desklamp grew talons
and perched like a tawny owl. Repelled by the gape
of blank paper, the pen's insinuations,
I ripped myself off from the bedsheets' sellotape,
donned the dead man's clothes, and made my escape.

Outside stretched a corridor with many doors
vibrating to a bass and drum thudded sound,
as if giant frogs leapt and belched beneath the floor,
over which keckled the white noise of a thousand
voices—all out of their heads. I could have swore
I lived in a terraced two-up two-down,
but on for a randyvoo, and keen to see you,
I opened the first door and walked straight through.

Half the town was in there, jam-packed and hot.
Johnny Tequila, his trousers much too tight,
tipped his bottle to my lips and didn't stop:
liquor-fire melting my defence against the night.
Huckle-bumped music grabbed at hips and didn't drop.
Glimmer-shimmered mirror balls spangled diamond bright.
It was a helter-skelter hell-raking hullabaloo.
But I moved on, for I couldn't see you.

In the next room I spent time with Johnny Trip
who split me into particles and scintilla,
entered my head, re-jigged its microchip
and left me in a garden of phlox and nicotiana
where electronic stars pulsed their beeps and blips
on nightgrass alive with ghost moths and cicadas
chasing anther-dust, their eyes bright orange moons.
But I couldn't see you, so I tried the next room.

I saw a ladder to heaven without any rungs.
I saw a truck speed through the night on fire.
I saw schoolteachers stalk schools with sawn-off shotguns.
I saw politicians sing *Imagine* in a naked choir.
I saw the allseeing eyeball of the sun
plucked from its socket in a tangle of wires.
I saw I was wigged-out and caught, in an endless queue,
between losing my place and looking for you.

On the stairs Johnny Debt was trading stocks and shares.
He read my accounts and hollered 'Here comes the rain!'
I asked if he had seen you anywhere?
but he just smiled and offered a payment plan insuring fear and pain.
He had a silver watch chain, gold mane of hair,
cocaine vial, old school tie. And shit for brains.
But I had to shake him off if I was ever to find
you, so I cursed my name upon his dotted line.

Johnny Fundamental was preparing for war.
He polished his boots, primed his weapons
and swore 'I'll kill until I die'. 'What for?'
I cried. But he picked up his machine gun
and quick-time marched out the door
shouting 'Johnny! Go! Go! Go!' Then he was gone
to make a blood sacrifice in the pine woods.
Oh Johnny find peace. Oh Johnny be good.

In the next room illegal aliens danced in cages.
Johnny Pimp made me swear to keep shtum.
Hand on heart he paid them honest wages.
He told me you'd been in my room,
but gurning over some scrunched-up pages,
had vanished quicker than an Irish summer's bloom—
faster than snow melts, in the blink of an eye,
you'd swept into the night like a mayfly.

In the next room I was detained for a week.
Monday I made up some parables and tales.
Tuesday the room hung upon each word I did speak.
Wednesday I burnt their money like a schlemiel.
Thursday I was hounded, branded, paraded as a freak.
Friday I got hammered. Absolutely nailed.
Saturday I was sarcophagized in a worm-crawling tomb.
Sunday I rose again and left that awful room.

The next room was a simulation console
for re-experiencing past mistakes.
Johnny Regret couldn't be consoled
and sadly sung a self-circling song for heartache
waiting to happen, which swizzled in my earhole.
Why are lost things the only things we can't break?
They manacled me, an invisible cage,
the unknown words I must have scribbled on that page.

Johnny Spliff asked 'You know when a tonal beat
repeats in a slow consistent rhythm
and draws you into the hypnotic secret
contained in each pulse, each drop in the ocean,
each star in space, so that chaos retreats,
or at least realigns into portioned design,
silk shot and mellow, shaped around
the mind and body's hinted fusion in that sound;

and then, when that simple rhythm quickens
and varies, tones broaden to chords,
the volume kicks in, and this calm pattern thickens,
wells up like a fizzy drink shaken to burst
through your inner walls with good vibrations;
then you flow in time with a wave's crest and crash,
all your particles flushed with the blush of a flower,
shouting *dah-dah!* in a Mardi Gras of colour;

then all the machines turn, like, organic, and hate U-
turns into hope that gushes through you, through-othered
with everyone else breaking free, riding their moment jackaroo
to that shuffle beat and crude clang and fuzztone clatter
so the undiscovered cosmos that rotates inside you
blows its wad and flops over
in a reamed steamed banana-creamed body-brain-blitzed howzat?
Well, why don't you write some words that work like that?'

At last I came to the final room—but I was not
out of trouble. For sitting there was Johnny Double.
He had re-written the scrunched-up note
you had read. He said 'Look, I helped you out—scribbled
a few gegs. So what? You were doing okay but got
bogged down in complicity with the world's troubles.
If someone huffs over words, it's their tough luck.
If you can't laugh, you're fucked.'

I jumped through the window. Down twelve stories I fell.
I ran for the road, but happened instead
upon a barbwire fence, on the other side of which welled
a harrowed queue of wraiths, groaning and wolf-eyed,
tattered and gowpen, clamouring to dwell
within—kept out by Johnny Border's thin red
line and armed guard, Alsatians and blowlamps,
his neat desk of paperfiles, inkpad and stamp.

I ran the rest of the night to a dew-soft lawn,
and on, into a wood of sycamore and pine
where I gashed through wild bramble as the slow-dawned
sky went gaga, glowing garnet and aquamarine,
while I thrashed through fernbrake and blackthorn
until the wood broke where coastal winds whined
and wheezed, the sky glummed, and the green-foamed
sea scunged to call its raindrops home.

Down raindrops plupped off the face of things and died.
From woven-coloured wood-shadows, Johnny Debt,
who'd trailed me ever since, sat down by my side,
put his arm around me, and together we watched wet
stragglers from the party trek their tired
way home on curving paths, becoming rainswept
and smaller, glistened blurs upon the leaze.
And now I know you won't come back to me

until the earth spins seven times around the moon;
until the clogged air clears and cools and breathes;
until there are no more busts and booms;
until the cows come home; you won't come back to me
until I learn to hold a tune;
until Icarus beats his wings and rises from the sea;
until the summer's in the meadow;
until the valley's hushed and white with snow;

until pigs fly, and water turns to whisky
or wine, and there's no more sour grapes;
until human nature is no longer a disease;
until we've free money, free love, and a free church in a free lay state.
And when you come, it's soft you'll tread above me,
but not until these falling nights abate
and I wake up, figure out what to do,
wanting to write a note perfect for you.

AUGUST IN EDINBURGH

Not a cloud in the sky and it's raining.
It's the brusqueness of things,
and the drag of things, that hurts.
The most beautiful woman in the world
is in Edinburgh, at the festival.
She looks me in the eye and says please
move I'm trying to look at the artworks.

My doctor says the heart works
but don't push it. I hear music,
long familiar songs, everywhere I go.
Pain is in the mind, someone tells Leonardo
DiCaprio in *Shutter Island*. Everyone
is rushing but the crowd moves slow.
Leonardo can't get his head around it.

A man in costume shouts we've sold out here
holding his hat out for money and rain.
The mind is an island and everyone
is beautiful, looking for something new
again. But nothing connects, and it's cold.
My son sticks my phone charger in his ear
and says I've got an electric brain.

I've been streaming old LPs I never thought
I'd hear again, never thinking the old songs
would not work, trying not to work the brain,
trying not to rise to the bait when that long
familiar voice rises from the damp and dismal
crowd, once again, to say hey, if we all think
hard enough, maybe we can stop this rain.

THE SCATTERING

Gone through the half-hearted window
that gives like a watery eye
onto the East, the blushlight of dawn
on scuzzed rooftops, scrolled hills;

gone over open-mouthed duck ponds,
decked lawns, a populace dreaming
of ordinary sex; gone with limitless texts
through the gridded air's dataflow,

the wheesht of elm leaves in the air,
a rustling blue polyester blouse;
gone with lost souls, their children
photostreams in the cloud,

indebted and encased in metal
and the motion of their cars past yellow
fields, roundabouts, the dead everywhere;
gone into the excitation of particles

and elements in contact with other
elements and particles like peedie
heads in a primary school playground
rushing away from fathers, mothers:

as I turn away, face the room I'm in,
half of me is already out the window
to chase and meet the scattering day
heading West, as if to say, well, hello.

LUNCH BREAK ON A BRIGHT DAY

If you lie on your back,
buck naked within your clothes,
under a beech or ash
tree's secluded grove

of park grass, letting
time pass with bird
nests above you
and a sound-quilt of bird

song about you,
as if in an alcove
looking up at a sun-spritzed
stained glass window,

watching the city's smoke
billow and waft
in delicate mallow puffs,
creamed meringue rafts

floating in the blue
lagoon sky,
you might come to suspect
the concourse between your eye

and brain,
for just like those old tubed
kaleidoscope toys you put
to your eye and turned

so everything went
Lucy in the Sky,
the sunlight wheels
and turns as you lie

within the umbra
of the tree
while the rinsing breeze
ripples the leaves

and sashaying twig-tips
with a shush
to the ear,
and each swish

of that green hair sprays the air
with glittered drops of bright
molten flushing amber,
lemon beads of light

in a river of glints,
a gush of glimmer-flow,
so you understand
the proposition *there is no*

fixed position
is now the only
fixed position,
for you can't take in this one tree,

the bark-brown
rutty dark of its bole,
its thick arms
upholding aureoles,

flavescent weavings,
branches sprouting
out of branches,
sprigs and spangs spouting

into a four thousand-
fingered trick of light,
pearl and honey
twinkling through slight

chinks between leaves,
glancing eyes through fronds,
micro-tints of ruby,
wet gleams of blonde

and bottle green,
leaf-tips like the lime
in a sharp tequila
and fizzed lime

soda sparkled with ice
trickling through a thin
multi-leaved
fluent-edged flim

of illuminated green
and aquamarine,
emerald, acid green,
avocado and margarine

until your head dances off
leaving you with luminance
in a haze of movement,
an overload of sense

and absence of reason
with which to rise
unsteady to your feet,
rub your twizzled eyes

and return to the city's
vast and hurried goad
of information flows,
firewalls, barcodes,

streets that give no pleasure
today when you walk, as you must,
back to work through the rot
and the rust and the ashes and the dust.

ZEITGEIST

I look for you behind retail parks,
ghost-lit showrooms, in dark
scrubland where plastics flutter on coils
of barbed wire; where, through mean soil
strewn with pipes, cartons, slugged condoms,
streams a steep-edged brook. Drawn
to its burble and splurge
I slip on the verge, fall and splunge
stretching for the banks, reeds, not catching hold
of anything sound, my hands ice-cube cold.
And past megastores, waste yards, the suburbs' borders,
carried along on colourless waters
ever gushing on, with no smile, no frown,
I call you down, I call you down.

City limits are fine but I spend most
days hemmed in, meshed and lost
up a tower—in front of a screen,
black plastic keyboard, black plastic machine
on a laminate desk—where the windows
won't open much in case I throw
myself out. Dust gathers on the phone,
empty plant pots. I am alone
much of the time to the extent
that a vague itch of harassment
prickles my contact with people.
And vacuumed through the non-soul
of blank matter, with no smile, no frown,
I call you down, I call you down.

Outside on shopped streets swarm mothers,
alpha males, screenagers, old, young, lovers,
the homeless, the bewildered, ill, unique,
the beautiful with their self-as-boutique—
so many, thronged into one body,
surrounding me, squishing, cumbering me
with sucken hair and grey breath,
a cracked open swallowing mouth.
And looking through a million eyes,
slouching upon a million thighs
compelled by the shackles
of meat-headed instinct to slowly circle
around and around, with no smile, no frown,
I call you down, I call you down.

Inside the machine or, at least, on the screen
I discover everything that has been,
will be, or might never be, has a place.
You can search for God, your name, any face
and reconfigure. You can hurt someone
and they won't know it was you. There's a room
for all things, the wall of each room an exit
to all that's possible, all interconnected
with, as they say, no edge and no centre.
I press enter and enter and enter
not knowing where to go, what I might find
in this flat expanding surveillant mind,
weightless, free floating, with no smile, no frown,
I commune. Then the machine powers down.

THE ESTATE

Blotches on walls and much dog
shit on pavements, hedges full of crisp bags,
chip bags and cans,
an eye at every window for the postman,
anyone at all, anything coming
or going, or unbecoming.

⌐

Well I couldn't stop cringing,
stuffing his face
with Monster Munch, like totally impinging
on my personal space,
and when I said so he was like look here missus
this here's a public bus.

⌐

An old fridge in the garden,
a boy showing his hard-on,
tracksuit bottoms pulled tight,
saying her tits were satellite
dishes, saying she burnt her ears on his thighs
with sullen eyes, sullen eyes, sullen eyes.

⌐

A flutter in the bookies and a fiver to put
before the wife. No football boots or
fresh fruit or computer
for the kids. No pay-per-view.
No suit
for a funeral, an interview.

⌐

Text sex, porno moans
in school corridors,
love rats on the floor
filming vajazzles on their phones.
Kylie's a dog. Tracey's a whore.
Ben has Simone groaning for his ringtone.

⌐

You queue and queue
for the intimidation of a too-
tidy desk, swanky office gear,
the bulletproof screen crystal clear.
Hello I'm here to kill you,
please sign here, here and here.

⌐

Don't be sayin but e thinks e's humungous.
On tha Viagra an then some, ah'm telling ya.
But sweaty balls. Fer Christmas e gave us
knickers that cut right inta
ma hole, an gave is fiancé Nigella
fuckin Lawson. Eh? Wha? Nah, she's gorgeous.

⌐

Sigourney was down to her knickers and vest,
the alien about to spring, when the fucking doorbell rings.
No the repo, but the Green Party canvassing.
I said I like your manifesto, put it to the test.
Oh go for a while with no cash flow no tobacco no quid pro quo
no Giro no logo no demo no lotto no blow no go no go no go no no no

SPRING

You might have butterflies
for no reason, all antsy
as if in anticipation
of the leaves' first look-and-see-me.

You might crack your nut trying to take in
the what of it, its here and this
while it lifts its skirts to brush by you,
fleeting past with one light kiss.

Bare-knuckled sycamores start wearing green.
Cherry blossom froths and pirouettes
in a brook, trickling past these streets
and estates, sloshing beneath tarmac,

visible here, underground there, everywhere
guzzling as the narrow-banked brook
rushes beyond scraggy reeds and weed tufts,
cacked plastics, sewer scurf, beer-can stooks,

streaming along in the green-glinted leaf-swish
and ripple of a petal-scented zing,
and with it flows all that we know of the here-
it-comes and there-it-goes of everything.

THE ALLEGORY OF SPRING

What pleasures we might find
 pass on.
Nothing to be done. Like air
 they are not long

to be held. Fast shadows darken
 fresh grass
and most of what we know
 grows bored

inside us. Like the sadness
 of money.
Like the measure of a median life,
 a McLife

like this one, rising to fall, falling
 to rise.
Yet here comes everyone—
 one by one

they peep their heads,
 creep out
from the dark to bud and spume
 like wild

fire into a teeming forest. There is
    something
mental about birth. You couldn't
    make it up:

the fury in seeds. Death not out-
    done. Death out-
doing us, our ceremonies,
    reaching

for the intangible, the way
    it drifts
like mist from a scalded
    teapot,

the tint of irises we never
    notice
in the vase, in the corner
    of the room,

until they're dying. Or that scent
    of moss
in the cover of the wood, creeping
    thistle,

greenfinches trilling in the brake
　　as if for us
on that walk I never wanted to take
　　then dreamed

about for nineteen years. Oh lay
　　me low.
Convolvulus and daffodils, the glissade
　　of beech leaves.

Lay me down in a shaded glade, though I
　　could count
the woods I've walked through in the past
　　nineteen years

on one hand and in that time
　　I must have
been to Tesco near four thousand times
　　taking four times

a week as a likely average. The soft prickle
　　of twayblade.
Fingers in the soil. Grass in the mouth.
　　Soft docken

leaves on buttercup-stained skin.
    What I like
best are garden centres, the calm trickle
    of their water

features, customers reverential
    in the ambience
of high ferns and pot plants. If we could rip
    the veil of habit,

witness the world truly, we would
    throw up.
And I hear their low moan, a woman
    and man

fucking in a supermarket
    toilet
because they've had it up to here. Hands on
    her buttocks

he tries to look the way he thinks
    he should
look, though his back hurts. Foxglove
    and may bells,

hair on willow-herb, nipples, genitals,
cellophane.
He hopes she's feeling what she should
be feeling.

She feels the muffled sorrow
and need
in the breath of pleasure. When he comes
she hugs him

but can't wrap herself around all
this plenty.
Done, they close their eyes and cradle
themselves

in that blindness. Then, as we all do,
hoping
for the best, they creep through the door
one by one.

THE RETURN

The next time I went home
I vowed truly to go home: one young one
head deep in the bloops and beeps of a phone

game, the other on a karaoke
microphone, her smile like piano
music with the wife hovering low-key

at the kitchen door, a grin on her mush,
saucepans frizzling. Before we settled down to it
I pulled the curtains against the brattle and whoosh

of the windows from the evening wind's gusts.
Later, the house quiet, I let
hot suds, once everything gleamed, suck and slush,

gargle into the hollow of the drain.
And in the dark hallway a hazy form
in the mirror asked who are you again?

THE FIELD

This lane can't help but lead
onto that lane I followed
when I was nine, stretched to green
fields from my aunt's farm
along this hedgeway that gives,
through a gap, to a blackthorn-guarded glade

where my catty older cousin says he'll drop me
from the roof of the cow barn onto the cows
if I don't follow the rules and chant
'Rise wormwood eyes' thirty-three times
with eyes shut so the dead can crawl
from the ground where they were murdered.

Sunlight streaks through the copse,
dribbles over honeysuckle;
a cabbage white flickers—a nervous
hand over black sloes; and under bridal-
white fluttering leaves I wheeze
'Rise wood dies' and half-open my eyes.

From the axe wound of a fungal
tree-stump they creep with bramble
fingers, bedstraw genitals, leaking hedge-

parsley. Light melts through their gaped
flowers, tongues of ret flax.
My hidden cousin wets his kecks.

My mother played in those feeding
grounds as a child before upping sticks
for the city. Staying at the house
of her birth for the holidays, my aunt
had proposed a picnic. And I would
follow the lane, enter the green field,

join those women in the meadow clover
and columbine, rings on their fingers
like marigolds, breaking fresh bread
but I shrink in the glade, waiting to be ravelled
with furze-brake and thorn-roots and to twist
for the rest of my days in this wake of the dead.

THE HOURGLASS

Time falls like rain
in the hourglass I keep turning over,
carried from the cupboard to your gingham-
covered deal table, trying to pother
the grains in your swept kitchen
on my first sleepover
at yours. You ask: 'One half empties, the other
fills. Now which half is happier?'

Both ends look dead by the end.
The hourglass shows how time gathers
but only lives through the movement of the sands.
Time suffocates the sphere it enters,
voids what it leaves behind.
Through a window the shadows of alders
jig across the room as you spool your reel
then roll in tinfoil two big tuna rolls.

Up before dawn so we can have lines in
the river for sunrise, the blanket
bog's surface glistens like fish skin
breathing in the moonlight.
I have read in *The Book of Great*
Facts that bogs don't grow, they accumulate
and I can believe it in my bobble hat,
borrowed twelve-eye boots and puffed jacket.

'Keep your eyes on your feet',
you say, 'this'll be the making of ye'.
Then a sudden sheep
gives me the skites and I slip on the scree
of the hill as it bleats
and shrieks, niddle-noddles its straggly
backside up the hillside
like a black-shawled old woman shaking her head.

Reaching higher ground I turn to look
back on the sweep of heather and sedge
quilting the slopes and sheughs
before we pass the high ridge
and traipse downhill to bait our hooks.
Lines ready at the slosh of the river edge
you turn to me in the sough of daybreak:
'Remember, take and give, give and take'.

Now time has spilled its darkness over you
I could say I'm back on those pitch
black fens once again, unable to
tell a hawthorn bush from a furzy ditch,
sludging to reach the stead of you
somewhere over the ridge
among shadows, sundews and fronds,
casting in the glent of the riverbend.

But I only stayed with you that one time
because of your drinking. Under a fleering moon
in a black-shawled night sky I dream
breathing sphagnum, moorgrass and broom
enter my body, like the taste of brine.
A cold shiver. How the rain and wide-roamed
dead, rivers and wilds, give and take,
hollow as they accumulate.

BEFORE WHAT WILL COME AFTER

Morning, when it comes, might ease the burden
the way McCandless, when I flipped him the bird in
1984 and he went buck mad altogether,
hunting me down like spleen-clouded weather
through the estate, up winding hill-lanes
into Killynether—hounding till we came

to thorn scrub where I got tangled,
snagged and haw-stained in bramble
as he viced me in a headlock, towed
me through green wood to an ash by the road,
the bracken in my ear an itching noise—
rubbed moss in my face, then yanked off my corduroys.

Morning, when it comes, might well stuff a thumb
in this seep of night-tremors, for what will come
could surely not outweigh the heavy night's
burden of waiting for it. Thinking back on it,
bar the cuts and bruises, it was a geg
the way McCandless hung my breeks, as if with pegs

on a line, on one of the ash branches
hung over the road, then fell on his haunches
and broke his hole laughing. Not that it felt

funny right then, I suppose: nettle welts,
aching arms, tree spleets poking at my thighs,
snatters streaming from nose and eyes.

Morning, when it comes, might snigger
the way Shonagh O'Dowd raised her finger
to McCandless, then split her smackers
at the sight of me in my undercrackers
dangled over the road, clinging to the tree,
as she drove past in her Ma's Mitsubishi.

I can still feel my raw hands lose grip
of the shaking branch, the breeze-trembled tips
of the leaves. I'm still trying to grapple
with the wood, my spinning head unable
to take in the slopes of overripe whin,
deep fields, blue lough, curved roads, all in a spin:

Shonagh O'Dowd a big-bellied teenage bride;
McCandless inside, then outside, then inside,
then scot-free altogether, to do harm
here and there, guns in McGilligan's farm
somewhere, wrapped deep in turnip fields;
her leaf-green eyes, all spinning like a flywheel.

My body aches, my ears buzzed with furze, stunk
by the night, sinking through the ash's trunk.
Her lying back in the ferns and harebells.

Him teaching me to smoke by the quarry's walls.
Laughter like bird noise, through the screeching leaves,
laughter in the night, in the pillow sleeves.

Morning, when it comes, will be welcome
as McCandless was when he helped me down
from the ash, grabbed my slacks, called me a tit
while I hoicked them back up on me by the pockets,
my ears huzzing, hiding my shaking hands
as we talked mushrooms, home games, bands,

the apple-flesh of Shonagh O'Dowd's thighs;
and I came alive in the sharpness of his eyes,
darting, ready to target what they could,
making our way back through that green wood
in lines straight as the woodcock's flight.
Morning may come, but this will be a long night.

SCAPEGOAT

After a botched job
on Cliftonville Road,
someone over-itchy on the trigger,
McCandless, his first job as driver, with a bloke
from another cell he doesn't know,
his anorak still spattered
with blood-smatter and boke,
is to hide on Scrabo Hill in a green
two-man tent that's light as a kite
with a bin bag of corned beef and baked beans—
be thankful for it ye gob-
shite—
until they figure
how to handle the matter.

Ah wis havin a cracker wee dream
lass night—there wis this wet thing
in mah ear. Then ah woke an seen
it wis a rat. At least a mouse.
Jesus, ah'm so cold ah'll go blind.
An ah swear ah'm gettin thin.
An if ah see one more fuckin tin
a cold baked bloody beans.
Could they nat ave bought Heinz?
Could they nat jus hide us in a house
in Ballybeen?
Christ, at this rate, if we wait
any longer it'll be nineteen
hundred and eighty-fuckin-eight.

McCandless adjusts to the night.
He stalks and creeps among high ferns
and purple loosestrife, cuts his shins on gorse,
munches on what he hopes is watercress
and clover, looking down at the town's
red, yellow, blue, white lights and slow cars.
In the sandstone quarry a black-winged
bird glides in circles under the cigar-
ring glows of stars. He etches *UFF*
on soft rock and risks sounding out
the echo of the quarry, startled
then dejected by the gulf of darkness
made more empty as the hill calls back to him:
FUCK OFF ... FUCK OFF ... OFF ... OFF ... FF ... F ...

Beneath the hill's turreted tower,
imperial man's fantastical cock,
McCandless looks over lego-
sized bungalows,
demesnes and estates
curved around
the tongue-tip of the lough,
the hard men of the town
burning late
in a rapture
of fear, visions of damnation,
internationalisation,
negro cocks,
rods, gag balls, Margaret Thatcher.

Jesus, ye don't talk much
do ye? We've been here how
long? Must be like forty
days an forty
fuckin nights by now
an next ta nuthin from ye—such
a big Mr Mystery.
Gie us yer share a tha corned dog
would ye? Skinny beardy
bastard. No fuckin odds
ah suppose. Yer too tight.
Christ, ah'm so hungry
ah could ate tha lamb ah god!
Jesus Christ could ye at least gimme a light?

McCandless scrunches a loose-stone path
under the new moon, scurries over spurge
on the bank, down into a barley field
sloping to meet the houses of an estate.
He peers through back windows at new kitchens.
A mousey-haired woman scrapes half-full plates
of potatoes into the bin and sighs
out at what must be her own reflection.
Looking for cracks in the curtains of bedrooms
he hits the jackpot: a young brunette yawns,
arches her back, unbuttons her blouse. He gawks
at the down of her armpits as she bunches
her hair and vanishes. The leash
of her bra strap. The coarse wet barley stalks.

On moonslicked fairways of the golf course
McCandless finds mushrooms. On all fours
he eats like a goat. Soon he's in a bunker
looking at stars. He sees myxomatized
rabbits staring hollow-eyed at nothing.
A Capri screeches across the putting green
with smashed bonnet, bullet holes in the windscreen.
A giant woman with the head of a frog,
the body of Linda Lusardi, peels off flesh-
coloured knickers, croaks in a broad brogue:
Now, you know you want to. He pounces
on a stray black dog in a quarry lane.
He holds it aloft, blood spilling
over him, yelling Who the fuck are ye?

Jesus, they're gonna kill me.
No doubt.
Gonna take me out.
Bury me under a tree
in Killynether.
But wha's bin tha point
ah makin us hang about?
Waitin fer never.
Ah could go an smoke whapper joints
in Florida an sell second hand
motors. Jesus, wid ye listen tah me?
Ah could go tah fuckin Scotland!
Christ, ah don't know.
Where you gonna go?

Come back to the tent at dawn
McCandless is unsurprised to find
himself alone, with no trace that someone
else has been there at all. All skin and bones
he lies down as mizzling rain fattens
to a downpour, thudding the tent walls,
his breath a brume in the fetid tent air.
With nothing to hit out at there's nothing
there. Surprised that he feels
his skull's been flipped open and he's been
filled to the brim with ashes
he touches his face, all matted beard,
grime, grease and pus, staring into
hollow green darkness. Ack, Jesus!

When they quietly climb the hill
with a gun and two shovels
they find nothing but a pile of barley seeds
on the tent floor. Spread out and look
one says. Another asks, what for?
If he's smart he's in Scotland.
But they hunt the hill's circle
until they go round the bend
convinced a furtive pair of eyes
looks out from every sycamore,
copse and covert, every clump of tall ferns.
They stop at the edge of Killynether.
On the coarse bark of an ash tree
is etched: *No Surrender*

FROM **A FURTHER DEFINITION OF MEMORY**

I had a mate called Snot
who had a sister called Chris
and their Da was shot
on 1st September 1986
(all names and dates have been altered).
Long ago, I'm sure, I forgot
the details and I don't consciously reminisce
but dream and dream again of that summer.

There were seven girls on our estate
and to follow the thread
of their chatter was to be reduced to a state
by seven bobbing heads
as they nattered—perched on low
walls or behind hedgerows
in McGarrigan's fields—headspun
and swept up by their twittered-chittered song.

You might say our town was a steaming brown
turd of a place with a Chinese, chippies,
graffiti, hairdressers, offies, closed-down
offices, bookies, more graffiti,
pool hall, nine pubs and video
library with posters of Chuck Norris videos.
On fair nights the seven girls perched in the town
square like birds. Twitching. Looking around.

On 31st August 1986
we headed for the duck pond,
the blushed sky tongued with scarlet licks.
Chris led me away from the rest
to the blue-tinged shelter of high fronds
and when she kissed me soft and long a
host of sparrows glided from the dark crest
of Scrabo over the vale of Kiltonga.

She raised herself, and I followed her under
hazels, down a path of wych elms,
their long shadows. I followed through a blur
of foxglove, columbine, tall ferns,
the trickle of a brook, under the whirr
of a far-off helicopter's rotors.
And now I hear the telephone ring
shrill and short the next morning,

the vacuum it brings; but right then
I followed her through dog-walk lanes,
scrub, empty fields and wasted glens
to where lead mines stretched for acres,
where we came across an old knacker
sat bolt upright on a deckchair
by an oil drum in the middle of nowhere
in particular, watching us draw near.

As we walked past in a slow motion haze
he mouthed an undecodable refrain
with hay in his beard and burning eyes,
spitting out his mantra again and again
in a fury of midges and horseflies.
And the discombobulation I felt in his gaze,
out of body and undermined,
was how I'd come to feel most of the time.

She kissed me, then walked off under darkened leaves
and I stood still, watching her leave.
And I wish she wandered broad and far
to that point on the horizon
where sky and sea become one,
where she wrapped the sky around her
like a blue cotton shawl and danced upon the waves.
But she went home to Ballycullen.

I've not been down that way since.
Nothing of those times can be changed
although their connotations constantly change
and I can't pin them down: my words like dust
as if ears of grain gleaned long before
by someone else, leaving only dry husks.
Do what I might, the mind implores
I stand there still, seeking a glimpse

of ribbon-braided hair. I reach out
and clutch at hollows—the telephone
ringing, red eyes, bilious refrains
in the ear, wilted columbine, foxglove,
fallen hazels, the constant spout
of a hidden brook purling through my brain.
And memory is looking on as love
walks off down a darkened green lane.

MORNING

To wake up is weird.
A clone of yourself,
you don't know where
you went, when you weren't here.
It looks like nowhere.

The night's storm of memories,
hex of dreams, has lifted.
A shower rinses you clean
again—good to go
on to the next night of memories, dreams.

Their interventions.
Moving on is more and more
like trying to reach an invented
somewhere you've already been.
To be there better than before.

You rush to catch your only bus
wishing you could enter the blue
day like a vast meterological
disturbance. But you do not pass
through life, it passes through you

the way the night passed
through on its way to who
knows where. And though it looks
like it has just come around,
that sun was already there.

ONE SUMMER MORNING

IN MEMORY OF RAYMOND POTTER

When you left
the house, where many were your guest,
on your last morning
I hope you stopped
on top of your steep steps
to take it in,
the bright field on the slopes
of the hill and the blue lift over the rooftops.

It isn't the ground we yield
that has us run away wild
through green fields
nor crows that sweep through the turned
sky over rivers as the crust
of the sun rusts on mild
estates and suburbs at dusk.
But how their image will burn.

Though nothing remains, still
that morning is where we might seek you.
A breeze blows in off the lough's blue.

A house sparrow flies into the cloud
as if on a mission.
Up steep steps, the slope of the shining hill,
would we find a note on the door:
Gone fishing!

RIVER MOUTH

If some regions of the brain are foreign
to others, as they say, this might explain
why my moods swing like hips in a hula dance:
now grumped, now chipper, now the essence
of cement, now a gushed river flow.
A woodland river. Green, brown and yellow
limn its banks: sprunt pines and bending sycamores,
song thrushes. It rushes for the shore
the way that urge surged through me, out my mouth
in sounds not half my own, when I burst forth
into song this morning in the kitchen.
There was no reason to sing. No one to listen.
Happiness comes on like a once-loved song
on the radio—played over in the mind once it's gone.
Useless to follow. It doesn't end, doesn't start:
a river that twists and turns into the unsatnaved heart
of the woods which shift in their shade perpetually,
sunlight pooling in the heads of the trees
while a congregation of sound fills the air,
pulls the ear. Useless to ponder where
that happiness went to, where it had been:
I can't even catch the dark-yellow-light-brown-flecked green
while I follow the many-voiced river through downs
and drumlins, rail stations at the border of town,

past warehouses, vast retail lots, car-stained
miles of suburban families detained
in dream homes. To apprehend such density
of life would be to hold fresh to memory
each page of each book on a full forty foot shelf.
The mind can't keep up with itself
and I get lost in town—masonry changed by whims
of weather, helter-skelter buildings on thin
streets huddled together: granite and whinstone,
polished ashlar, red sandstone, blonde and brown stone,
many-sized windows numerous as rain-
drops in the air, each an eye cast on this drained
world, each an eye giving onto an inner
realm I peer into, staring at the décor
of strange rooms, going 'ooohh', 'yuk', or 'hmm?',
catching a glimpse of a grey cluttered room:
a woman at a desk, rubbing her aching neck,
her tired eyes, turning away from her book,
laptop, stacked plates and cups, scribbled words,
turning away from this tasked world towards
an inner realm: her thoughts like quicksilver shoals
in motion through a green water-blue soul,
her eye a twilight moon over this wood's
gushing river that I follow under the mood
swings of sycamores, fearful of the pines,
wondering where on earth does the time
go while the weather turns and cold winds

ruffle the witch hazel, rustle the whin,
wilting sweet gum. Smokebush withers.
Woodland thins. Crows caw and circle
the blush sky, mild above autumn's
mown fields, borderlands, foreign regions
where the river, many rivers, empty
into a dark sea, the mind of nobody
where whatever it was that was borne in song
floats and dims on the brim of meaning.

NIGHT SONG FOR ROSIE

Look up at the night's wide dome
adrift through the calm of your mind,
an open vat of deep silent wine—

like floating on the lakes of the moon—
reflecting stars, a looking glass of dreams,
your eyes, upon noiseless waters.

These waters will evaporate and rise,
stew and frown into stormy weather
to murk the stars, darken your eyes.

This will come. This will go. Rest your mind,
pressing down, light unto a screen.
Don't let yourself be tormented.

The stars are grapes swelling on a vine,
aching to fall, to be fermented
in the Lake of Softness, Lake of Time.

THE SWEEPING

When you're cobwebbed,
        your head's stale bread,
batteries low as can go;
        when all you might say
slubs your mouth and dulls to clay:

get yourself outdoors
            when the weather turns mean.
    I mean
when gravid howl-soon scum clouds,
           big bad bruised bastards,
fat soiled swollen arses plunged
           down the scuzzed bowl of the sky
gather and gulder in hordes
      like thugs-for-hire far too keen on their jobs,
as if there was terror in heaven,
         as if a dark angel might render
         a cumulonimbus-shaped
megaphone to dictate a contract of surrender:
         'Abide by our terms and you will learn
       of the ecstasy that burned in Job
     as he shaved his head, threw himself
upon the ground and worshipped'.

Get yourself outside to suck
                    up the calamity
          of hound-black howlers
huffed up over the frazzled nerve-
                    ends of needle-furze,
thrawn wheat, barley, maize, bulrush,
                    over the motion-sick
surface of fast-frumpled reservoirs,
          discomfuffled lakes,
frothing loughs, scampering rivers
          that will soon break
their banks, scuttled poons,
                    elms and larches convulsing in the air
                    like headbangers' hair
in the throes of death
                    metal music.

Get yourself flubbed and freaked
                    by screamers that fly at
          your senses, sidewinders in a riot
of knuckle-dustered
                    blow-you-four-ways
superfuzzed nutter-gusters,
                    and prepare to get nailed
          as the sky rips
its strained skin to begin
                    its belly-ache,

bowel-shift and waterbreak,
        a hissed dissle
            growing into
            a trillion-splattered sizzle
                growing into
                a zillion form-seeking missiles
of water a minute
            launched in a bungalow-
                battering crescendo
of hard clots and ingots of hail
                that the dust, dirt, mire
        and loan gollop
until the ground parts
            as if with parting
legs to fart loose dirt-dregs,
                a glair and squelch,
                ooze and dreel
of curdled quags
            gubbled and squinnied
in hinnying gallops
                of pelleted rain,
        flinty sleet-splatters that mawl
and serrate the sculpted
suburban hedges,
            smash the manicured lawn-
grass, gnash the lady's smock,
                slash the foxfire,

thrash junipers and elders
in a scatter of sprays,
        sprigs and tatters.

Let rain scrub the scroofy walls
                of banks, bookies, bars,
        detached houses,
corner shops,
        their soot-scunged windows;
let rain dance stocious on rooftops;
                let rain riddle and ding
the bonnets of sprootzy-dootzy cars,
                now scrunted and stricken;
        let rain sluice and juice spew-
pools of coagulated chicken
                nuggets, vodka jellies,
                overspilling belly-busted
back-alley bin-bilge,
                heaving nidorous hunks
        of over-thwunked milge;
let rain scutter and whang
        the scudded cronk
                and slag of industrial yards;
                let rain water-cannon
goose shit, lucerne,
                scumber from farmyards
and swish and swill in potato
        drills;

let rain slish down on sileage,
                    bones and ammonia;
          let rain scour clean the vents
and sills of haggard hills,
                    the land you stand on,
the greywacke, siltstone,
                    saltmarsh,
          the seizure of the shore.

And when you look up to see
                    gashed light through the thunder-
          head feeling
gingerish in thaw-rain,
                    skin-raw, dirled and dinted,
flenched, pogo-brained, infinitesimal,
                    flushed out
in thrall to the after-din
          and after-fall,
you can come back inside,
          flurred and flummoxed but unbleared,
                    rinsed to the hollows,
                    uprooted and reeling
          yet circumfluent.
Good to go.

NOTES

"12th October, 1994": On 13th October, 1994 the "Combined Loyalist Military Command" announced a ceasefire in Northern Ireland.

"Bob the Builder Is a Dickhead": "On the threshold of heaven, the figures in the street / Become the figures of heaven," from Wallace Stevens's "To An Old Philosopher in Rome."

"Laganside": The penultimate stanzas of "Ovid in Tomis" by Derek Mahon read: "Better to contemplate / The blank page / And leave it blank // Than modify / Its substance by / So much as a pen-stroke. // Woven of wood nymphs, / It speaks volumes / No one will ever write."

"*from* In Whose Blent Air All Our Compulsions Meet": The title is from Philip Larkin's "Church Going." The three "partly-scrubbed street slogans" presumably read in their original form: "Vote for Sinn Féin," "Fuck the Pope," and "God is Good."

"The Green Rose": Quotations from Whitman's "Song of Myself."

"Scapegoat": Corned beef is idiomatically termed "corned dog." Linda Lusardi was a prominent glamour model in the British tabloid press throughout the late 1970s and the 1980s.